THE TOLTEC WAY

THE TOLTEC WAY

A GUIDE TO PERSONAL
TRANSFORMATION

DR. SUSAN GREGG

RENAISSANCE BOOKS
New York

Note: Rather than use the masculine gender to denote both men and women, we have used "he" and "she" randomly throughout the text.

www.stmartins.com

ISBN 1-58063-214-9

Design by Lisa-Theresa Lenthall

First Paperback Edition: September 2001

10   9   8   7   6   5   4   3

This book is dedicated to that spark of energy that gives us life and to the concept of personal freedom. May we all learn to live in dominion, love unconditionally, and remember our divinity.

ACKNOWLEDGMENTS

I would like to thank my agent Sheree Bykofsky and all the wonderful people at Renaissance Books who made this book possible.

I want to thank all my students for their love and support. I want to say a special thanks to Chuckie for asking me to start teaching in the first place. To my teachers, don Miguel and Sister Sarita, thank you seems so inadequate. To Tony, my mentor and friend, thanks for helping me find myself. My heartfelt thanks to my parents. Dad, thanks for believing in me even when I couldn't. And Mom, thanks for the curly hair and all your love.

I also wish to express my gratitude and my love to those closest to me. I give my deepest thanks to all my wonderful fur children who constantly remind me of all the joy life has to offer. To my love, I thank you for your patience, guidance, and support while I lived at my computer.

My special thanks goes to my creator for blessing me with another chance to remember and for the opportunity to be of service.

And a hearty thanks to you the reader for picking up this book. May you use the knowledge in it to set yourself free.

Namaste

CONTENTS

FOREWORD

Susan Gregg's *The Toltec Way: a Guide to Personal Transformation* is a recapitulation of the techniques and procedures we did together more than ten years ago. The practices served as a guide for her incredible spiritual growth.

Her life was completely transformed. Susan found the strength and courage to face all the fears and beliefs that used to guide her life into drama and emotional pain.

Susan practiced these techniques every day for many months until they became a new habit in her life, until she mastered a new life. Her life no longer was in drama but became one of happiness, joy, and love.

Her gratitude for that transformation is so great that Susan has decided to share everything she learned with whomever wants to take advantage of her mastery. She has decided to take apprentices of her own, to guide them to personal freedom as I did with her.

I am so happy to see how all of her apprentices have the benefit of her love. I feel so happy to see the success of her first two books. This new book holds the keys to transformation. If you decide to practice these techniques, they will guide you to your personal freedom, to your happiness, to your self-realization.

—don Miguel Ruiz

THE TOLTEC WAY

PART ONE

The Toltec Tradition

The Toltecs flourished as a civilization in southern Mexico around A.D. 900. They were a rather violent society that introduced militarism to Mesoamerica, but they also were known as master builders and craftsmen. Their stone figures are magnificent. After they conquered the city of Teotihuacan, a secret society formed within their civilization that was dedicated to preserving the knowledge of the ancient ones. The ancient ones were a race of people who were teachers of spirituality, science, and the arts. This secret society embraced the ideals of priestly rule and peaceful behavior that the city was known for, and they later became known as "men and women of knowledge."

According to the Toltec, the ancient ones understood the illusionary nature of reality and were able to use the universal laws of nature to create a life based on unconditional love and self-discovery. They considered all of life to be part of a great mystery and knew there was no way to separate the secular from the sacred or science from spirit. To a "normal" person, they appeared to be magicians or wizards; they could perform great feats, heal the sick, and create whatever they wanted. They could also transform matter.

The Toltec preserved this knowledge and taught it to their apprentices. After the Spanish conquest, the knowledge became a carefully guarded secret passed down through various lineages. Today, this information is again being shared more openly.

The Toltec tradition is a wonderful journey, a journey in which you will find yourself and have the opportunity to re-create your life. It is a guide and a blueprint for living that shows you how to experience life in a limitless manner. It will show you how to make profound, permanent changes in your life. And it will help you remember your ability to create whatever you want, whenever you want it.

CHAPTER ONE

My Introduction to the Toltec Way

I remember the night I started my journey. I had no idea where it was leading, but I knew I had to follow the path magically unfolding before me. And what a magnificent journey it has been.

I have always *known* at a core level that life could be easy and effortless and filled with joy. However, before my philosophical studies, my life was far from easy. I was working at a job that gave me no fulfillment and I experienced a great deal of drama, pain, and struggle. At times, I thought that life was not worth living and thought about suicide. Then I met a Mexican Indian named don Miguel Angel Ruiz. Don Miguel is a charismatic Toltec Master and *nagual* (one who guides an individual to personal freedom). I went from being chronically depressed, lonely, and generally miserable, to a person who lives life passionately and is joyful most of the time. Today I enjoy what I do and my life is filled with love and magic. My life now is far better than anything I could have ever imagined. As you gain this new perspective and exert a little discipline and dedication, anything is possible.

I had lived in Vermont for over twenty years and I was tired of the cold, so I decided to move to California. I settled in San Diego in the fall of 1986. Within a few days I met an older woman named Mary who took me under her wing. When she met me she announced to anyone who would listen that I was a powerful healer and teacher. I figured that she was just a typical West Coast resident.

One evening, a few weeks later, she suggested I join her in the barrio to meet a friend of hers named Sister Sarita who was a very well-known healer. It was a rainy evening in late September. The wind was coming in off the ocean making the air feel cool. I could taste the salty air on my lips and smell the sweet scent of kelp.

Trying to stay warm, I paced impatiently, nervously awaiting my friend outside the clinic where we were to meet. When she arrived, we walked into a place she called "the temple." Actually, it had been a Laundromat; there was a large and colorful painting of an eye surrounded by a triangle painted on the front window. At the front of the room was an altar enclosed by faded purple velvet curtains. An assortment of glass jars held bouquets of mums and gladiolas in various stages of decomposition. Even though the surroundings were old and dingy, the atmosphere was vibrant and alive, almost magical. People gathered in small clusters, speaking with animation in Spanish.

Mary took me over to meet Sister Sarita, who spoke rapidly to Mary. She then smiled at me and embraced me warmly. She looked pleased. Mary and I found a seat and I sat there waiting; I had no idea what to expect. As Sister Sarita stood and lovingly looked around the room, the crowd quieted. She said a beautiful prayer in Spanish; her voice was hypnotic. Even though I couldn't understand the words, I could feel the gratitude and the love she was expressing.

After she finished the prayer, she and her students began moving around the room. I had never seen anything quite like it. It looked like an ancient ballet—gentle, graceful movements in slow motion, pauses, and then rhythmic movement again. I watched intently, feeling slightly confused and out of place.

A man with intense, dark eyes approached me and motioned for me to step into the center of the circle. I wasn't sure what he wanted, but somehow I had the feeling he wanted me to perform a healing on him. It was like an inner knowing; I'd never felt anything like that before. I stepped forward, watched the other students for a moment, and then felt guided to make a series of movements around his body. I started at his head and made sweeping motions. At times I felt guided to merely hold my hand over certain areas of his body. When I was done he smiled at me, nodded, turned, and then he walked away.

Before I had time to sit down, the man returned and stood in front of me with a young woman. She translated for him. He said he wanted me to become his student and, without hesitation, I said yes.

I was shocked that I had agreed. Part of me thought I had lost my mind but I knew this was something I had to do. Little did I know that the next three years of my life would be totally consumed by my studies with don Miguel and his mother.

Saturday night of that same week found me back at the temple. It was a small group, and Wanda, the woman who had translated for don Miguel, sat next to me. Sister Sarita, don Miguel's mother, spoke rapidly in Spanish. I listened half to her and half to Wanda as she translated Sister Sarita's words. I had a hard time understanding what was being said: The Toltec concepts of energy and responsibility and God seemed so foreign. Much of it made no sense to me at all.

At the end of the class we sat in a circle and meditated. Don Miguel got up and moved around the room. He would pause in front of each person, moving his hands around their bodies without touching them. His behavior was very deliberate but confusing to me. I felt something in my body when he stood in front of me, but I didn't know what to think. Later, I learned he was directing the energy, assisting people in opening up.

I began rearranging my life so I could spend as much time as possible with Sister Sarita and don Miguel. Sister Sarita's father had trained her in the Toltec tradition, and they both passed the knowledge down to don Miguel. He in turn passed it on to me. The Toltec knowledge had been kept in secrecy for hundreds of years but Sister Sarita and don Miguel felt guided to share the powerful teachings with others.

When I began studying with him, don Miguel spoke very little English and I spoke no Spanish. For a long time I had no idea what I was studying, but something deep inside of me just knew I needed to be there. I was amazed that I continued to show up week after week. Normally my thinking was very rational and linear, particularly as my educational background was in math and physics. Repeatedly showing up at the temple for no logical reason was out of character for me. Sometimes in the middle of the day I would find myself drawn to the temple and don Miguel would be sitting there, almost as if he'd been waiting for me.

I spent a great deal of time with Sister Sarita watching and learning as she healed people. She was always patient and loving with me. One day an old man came into the temple with an unsightly, festering sore on his leg. Sister Sarita asked me, in Spanish, for an egg. I had no idea what she was saying. She kept holding up both of her hands in an oval shape. I must have handed her everything oval shaped in the temple. Finally I heard a voice come over the partition saying, "She wants an egg." I ran upstairs to where they stored flats of eggs and brought her one. Eggs have been used for centuries by Mexican healers or *curanderas* to clear a person's energy field.

When I finally handed her an egg, she laughed and proceeded to heal the man's leg. After several minutes, the wound on his leg disappeared. I would walk away from sessions with her in a state of utter bewilderment. What I had seen just wasn't possible. I was shocked when I learned that Sister Sarita was in her late seventies, as she looked so much younger and so vibrant.

Due to the language barrier, I couldn't ask don Miguel any in-depth questions about what we were doing. In retrospect I realize what a gift that was; it prevented me from engaging my mind and analyzing what was going on. With my mind detached, I fully experienced the moment. There were many times I would ask him what to do or what something meant. I always wanted to know if I was doing it right. He never answered. No matter what I asked, he would just smile and nod his head. We spent a great deal of time out in nature. I learned to concentrate on what I was feeling in my body rather than on what I was thinking. Even after he learned to speak English, he wouldn't really answer my questions. He would just smile at me and nod his head. Eventually I realized that that smile meant I was about to experience something that would cause me to question what my mind called my sanity.

I realized that my mind had a limited way of looking at myself and the world around me. As I continued my studies I began to identify my true nature, which was a spiritual energy residing within a body. As I changed my focus from my mind (my reason) to my spirit (my will), my limitations fell away and my life began to change. I began to live a life based on personal freedom; happiness became a matter of choice.

The changes were not always easy and were often emotionally challenging. To be honest, during the course of my training I often felt victimized by the changes occurring in my life. My old way of living stopped working long before I knew that there was another way. Over the years I found that each of us has our own unique path, but at that time I was still questioning, and searching for my own.

In my first book, *Dance of Power,* I talk at length about the challenges the path to freedom presents. Recently a woman who read it asked what had stopped me from throwing my hands up in frustration and saying "I quit." As she read my books she kept thinking, "If that had happened to me, I would have quit." The best answer I had for her at the time was that I somehow knew I had no choice but to continue on my quest for my true self. Quitting just wasn't an option.

A few days after the woman and I spoke, I had an insight into my process that I'd like to share. I was meditating in the sanctuary of a Catholic Church. When I opened my eyes, a group of children were coming out of the back room. All, except one, were bouncing along. One little boy was very solemnly carrying a bottle of oil. He reverently walked along in silence. He seemed to understand the sacred nature of the act that was about to be performed.

His face was filled with peace, the peace one finds after the emotional wounds from the past are healed. He reminded me of all the people I had seen quit just before they made that breakthrough. That profound, sacred connection is such a gift and the clamoring noise in our minds stops us from feeling that connection. I wondered if he would be able to hold onto his sacred connection or if he would lose it as he grew older. I was filled with a sense of gratitude that I had taken the time and made the effort necessary to renew that connection as an adult. It allowed me to stay the course even when the going got rough. What an incredible life I would have missed if I hadn't.

As I continued to meditate, I wondered why I had gone on when so many others would have quit. Over the years I've seen so many people walk away from their path right before they were about to have a major breakthrough. At the moment they're about to experience a miracle, I've seen people convince themselves that they need to do something else, or they need more time for themselves, or ... the reasons are endless. What stopped me from doing that?

Sitting near a statue of Jesus, I began to wonder what he did, how he achieved personal freedom. I felt that his personal freedom was rooted in a deep sense of love and compassion for himself and others. I know we all need to be gentle with ourselves; we need to accept our process and honor where we are before we can move forward. Love and compassion are far better motivators than fear and judgment.

I realized that great teachers such as Buddha, Lao Tse, and Jesus were completely dedicated to experiencing and sharing their divinity. During the course of their lives, they had made certain behaviors non-negotiable. They prayed and meditated on a regular basis. They did whatever it took to maintain a deep and clear connection to their spiritual selves. That connection became like the very air they breathed, a non-negotiable part of life.

In my classes I often talk about the need for discipline and dedication, two words we hate to hear. Enlightened beings like Jesus, Buddha, and Lao Tse had the discipline to overcome any obstacle. They saw themselves as God had created them rather than as their minds perceived themselves. They knew God was an energy that gave them life and not an external being that judged them. From direct experience they knew God was all-loving; they knew the universe was a friendly place.

When I finished my meditation, I realized that I had a much clearer answer for how I'd managed to continue. I made certain things in my daily life non-negotiable.

Shortly after beginning my studies, I placed a small, white index card in the corner of my bathroom mirror with a list of four items. I remember many nights getting out of my warm bed to finish my list of non-negotiable tasks. The first was to stand in front of the mirror, look deeply into my eyes, and talk lovingly to myself twice a day. The second was to go to the beach and pray, the third was to meditate, and the fourth was to write in my journal.

I prayed and meditated daily. I had a loving mentor in a twelve-step program I attended who told me to find a place I could talk to God and go there every day. Every morning I went to the beach and prayed to feel the love in the world. I would open my heart and let that love in, then I would go about my day.

I did my best to maintain an attitude of humility. Whenever I was unsure of what to do or how to do it, rather than guessing, I would say, "I don't know." As soon as I made this admission, I became teachable and the answers would come. When I felt totally hopeless and didn't want to go on, I remembered that quitting wasn't an option.

I never allowed myself to stay in bed and put these things off until tomorrow because, after all, doing them was non-negotiable. Non-negotiable means no room for negotiation, none whatsoever.

I made my studies non-negotiable. If don Miguel suggested I do something, I did it. I dedicated myself to achieving personal freedom. During my studies, many people came and went. They got out of the classes exactly what they put in. Very few people are willing to do whatever it takes to achieve personal freedom. Personal freedom does have a price, but believe me, it is well worth the effort.

After many years of studying with don Miguel, one afternoon we went whale watching. As the sun was setting, he told me that he had taught me all he could. He gently held my hand, looked lovingly into my eyes, and told me it was time for me to go and teach in my own way. Several weeks later he performed a ceremony for me in which he declared that I was a Woman of Power, a Toltec Master. My time of searching externally had come to an end and I knew then, without a doubt, that I could only find my answers by going within.

Shortly after that, I moved to Hawaii and started working as a counselor. I began searching for ways to share these powerful truths with others and since the mid-1980s I have been assisting people in breaking free of their limitations. I quickly realized that most people don't want to spend years studying an ancient tradition to improve the quality of their life, nor is that necessary. What is necessary is a willingness to see yourself and the world around you with new eyes—and a great technique for learning to do so is through the teachings of the Toltec people.

To introduce the Toltec methods, I've divided this book into five parts. The first part will give you an overview of the Toltecs and their beliefs. The next three parts will focus on attaining the three Toltec Masteries: Awareness, Transformation, and Intent. The last part will explore various aspects of maintaining the new perspectives you have achieved. At times, you will probably be confused and frustrated by some of the concepts in this book, but as you learn to use the tools provided, you will find yourself coming to a greater understanding. And you will develop the ability to be happy regardless of the events in your life. You will learn to love yourself, others, and life at a very deep level.

You will find some of the most important knowledge in the teaching stories scattered throughout this book. The wisdom of the ancient ones was often passed on in the form of stories, as we do not always have adequate language to convey its meaning directly. When I studied with don Miguel I learned that the stories, the exercises, and the knowledge he shared with me in an unpremeditated manner were often the most valuable. It was my job to pay attention. If I asked a question, we would talk about my concern but he wouldn't raise the issue again unless I did. Read the stories, do the exercises, and allow the wisdom of the ancient ones to speak to your heart so you can reconnect with your true self.

As you read this book, it is important to give yourself permission to learn and to relax and trust the process. Meditating is a good way to practice those skills, and so I've included an appendix of guided meditations. A very effective technique is to record the meditations and play them back to yourself. By doing so, you won't need to be reading and visualizing at the same time. Or, have a friend with a soothing voice record them for you.

In these meditations, you'll be asked to visualize scenes, people, or events. Everyone can visualize, and because we all visualize differently, there is no one correct way to do it. Don't be concerned that you're not visualizing "well enough." If your visualization has an elusive quality, that's just fine. Allow yourself to play with the idea and have fun. Make it a game. Sure you'll be skeptical at times, and maybe even a little daunted. This journey is, to be truthful, somewhat arduous. It is not made overnight but is a process that can take some time.

Question your old beliefs; be willing to suspend judgment. You learned to walk by falling down. If you had refused to allow yourself to fall down, you never would have learned how to walk. Give yourself permission to learn. Give yourself permission to be awkward and unsure.

I had doubts and reservations the entire time I was studying with don Miguel and Sister Sarita. I just didn't act on them. Even when I experienced profound healings, my mind would tell me I must not have been really injured or sick in the first place. Much of the information in this book will make little or no sense to your rational, linear mind, but I can guarantee that if you apply it to your life, your life will be completely transformed.

CHAPTER TWO

An Ancient Understanding

The Toltec believed that if we understand the microcosm, which is ourselves, we will understand the macrocosm, which is the universe. The inner and outer worlds mirror each other. We can stand outside on a dark night, surrounded by billions of stars, and be completely unaware of our connection to everyone and everything in our universe. In the same way, an electron within our body can be surrounded by billions of atoms and molecules and like us, that electron doesn't know it is part of a complex organism called the body. It sees itself as separate from the rest of the atoms. It doesn't realize that it is one with the rest of the body and that for the organism to remain healthy, all of its cells must remain in harmony. The Toltec viewed the macrocosm, and everything in it, as a complex energy system.

On the physical level, as we understand it, everything is composed of atoms. Physicists have found that if they split the atom far enough, they find pure energy. According to quantum physics, waves and particles act in very different manners. When an atom is split, if the observer expects the energy to act like a particle, it will; if the observer expects it to act like a wave, it will do that, too. Since energy responds to the beliefs of the observer, it must be able to perceive what the observer is thinking. Quantum physics has proven what the Toltec masters have known for hundreds of years: that all energy has consciousness.

When energy is experienced at a pure level, that state of consciousness is expansive, non-judgmental, and unconditionally loving. It is infinite, immortal, universal, and all-inclusive. At this level of energy we are all one; there is no separation or duality. The teaching story that follows this chapter speaks to the experience of energy at this pure level.

On the microcosmic level, the human body contains many different kinds of cells. A skin cell isn't aware of the existence of a liver cell, but all the cells must function together properly or the entire system is in jeopardy. On a global or macrocosmic level, we are cells of the earth and the earth is a cell of the universe. We are all part of that magnificent energy. And just like the cells of our body, when we are out of harmony with that energy, not only are we are out of balance, but we also send that imbalance out to others. We forget how powerful we are—that we can create diviseness for the world to mirror or we can create a place within the world for love to grow.

Many philosophies discuss the microcosm and the macrocosm. Most people are familiar with the idea that we are all one, so what makes the Toltec tradition so different? The Toltec Masteries not only allow you to know that the world is a vast energy system, but will teach you how to experience that for yourself. When you sit at the very core of your being, look at the world, and see it as a vast energy system, the world becomes an entirely different place. You no longer wonder about feeling safe or what to do next; you just follow the energy and know, beyond a shadow of a doubt, that you are one, you are perfect, you are God. Once you are aware of your true nature, the universe becomes a friendly, supportive, nurturing place in which to explore and grow.

The Toltec sense of the relationship of each of us to the macrocosm is unique because it is experiential. Once you begin to practice the three Masteries in your life, you are not contemplating a theory, you are experiencing a oneness with everything moment by moment on a daily basis.

Anyone who uses the tools and follows the precepts of the Toltec tradition can experience energy at its pure level and create a life of limitless possibilities. This tradition is not a religion; it is a way of life. Its gift is the attainment of personal freedom. Simply put, personal freedom is the ability to choose how to *act* rather than *reacting* to the events in our lives; it is the ability to be happy no matter what. This freedom is achieved by shifting our consciousness, by seeing the world as it really exists—and by transcending what we perceive as our limitations.

The three Toltec Masteries of Awareness, Transformation, and Intent work hand in hand with each other to help you access the inner wisdom that will allow you to lead a life based on love and joy. They are tools that will assist you in stepping fully into the present, so that you can choose moment by moment what it is that you want to create. They will, with discipline and dedication, allow you to become aware of your own divinity.

The first mastery is Awareness: It is the ability to see with clarity. Next you must learn to Transform yourself: You must thoroughly understand all of the assumptions, agreements, and beliefs you have about your problems in order to know what to change. Finally you will learn to use your Intent to help you focus your attention so you can be the peaceful, harmonized person that you want to be.

Although the Masteries are set forth in a sequence, this presentation is only marginally accurate. The Masteries are very much interwoven and you don't attain one, stop, and then attain another. Try to bear in mind that the path through the Masteries will wind, and at times seem to re-trace itself. The layered texture of the Masteries is troublesome to many of us as it doesn't comply with our linear way of thinking. Much of this book is about changing the way we think, and accepting the winding ways of the Toltec Masteries is part of the process.

Think, right now, this very second, of all the things that ran through your brain as you read this page. To what extent was your attention on the text? Did you have any other thoughts at the same time, such as: "What is this author talking about? Did I leave the front burner on?

This paper cut's annoying. How, if I'm broke until payday, am I supposed to create what I want at that moment?"

This constant "chatter" is what the Toltec called the *mitote* of the mind. The *mitote* is the symphony of voices always clamoring for your attention, all the opinions, thoughts, and ideas that constantly whirl around in your mind. Beyond that endless noise is a place of silence, a place of peace. When we learn to live our lives from that place we can be happy no matter what is happening around us—and we can live our lives based on love, free of fear, stress, and anxiety. With the wisdom of the Toltecs, the *mitote* can be silenced.

TEACHING STORY

Living in Love / Living in Fear

The clouds were still pink and orange from the last rays of the sun. You could see people's breath as they moved rapidly through the village. It would be another cold night. The musky smell of piñon wood floated up from the cooking fires and the sound of children's laughter filled the air.

The Grandmother sat in silence watching and waiting. Her heart was filled with love as she looked down upon her village.

Soon the children would gather about her feet, clamoring for their evening story. How she loved their curiosity and their innocence. They questioned everything not because they were cynical but because they were sincerely curious. That was why they learned so easily. Curiosity and openness pushed them to question and to learn. It was their gift to all who cared to notice. Adults could learn much from children.

Years ago while she was caring for two of her young charges a young boy asked to hold his infant sister. It was an unusual request so she asked the boy why. He looked at her very solemnly and replied, "Because she is closer to the Great Spirit and I am beginning to forget." She handed him his sister and watched. He spent hours looking into her eyes. Now he's a great healer and teacher in a village far away.

"What would you like to hear about tonight, children?"

There was a great deal of laughter and whispering. They had been trained to confer among themselves and come up with a single request. After a time the smallest girl stood up and announced they would like to hear of their future.

The Grandmother laughed and looked solemnly at each of them. Then she closed her eyes and began to speak.

"One of you will be a great chief, one of you a thief, while one of you will be a powerful healer. Among you there will be mothers and husbands that are good providers. There will be good hunters and bad ones. But each of you, no matter what you become, is part of the Great Spirit. You are not what you do or who you become. You are a light, a shining example of the love the Great Spirit placed inside each of us."

"But Grandmother, who among us will be the chief and who will be the thief?"

"Why does that matter little one? The Great Spirit wants us to treat all of his children the same, with love and compassion.

"A great chief loves the healer and the thief. Perhaps he even loves the thief just a little more because he is wounded and needs his love in order to heal. Only love heals. Anger, hatred, and judgment only create deeper wounds."

"I don't understand, Grandmother," said the oldest boy. "If someone steals something of mine I would be very angry."

"Why?" asked the Grandmother. "Do you fear there will be no more? Is not everything but a gift to be shared? If you give love in return for betrayal, have you really been betrayed? And is anything except love real?

"Remember, anyone who shares anything but love is wounded and must be treated with compassion.

Love and compassion will set you free and they might just heal the heart of the thief."

Off in the distance voices were calling the children for dinner.

"Now go and think about the words you have heard. Think about the incredible power love has to heal and ask yourself which you want to guide your life, love or fear?"

CHAPTER THREE

A Modern Interpretation of the Toltec Path

I've infused don Miguel's Toltec teachings with the feminine principles of harmony and spirituality. I am part of the lineage of what I have come to call the new seers. The ancient Toltec seers were right: We are a spiritual energy contained within our physical bodies. I also believe, however, that all energy is one and makes up the totality of the energy we call God. As a new seer, I know we live in a universe that is totally safe, loving, and supportive, and I have found that the greatest benefits from the Toltec Masteries can be drawn from this perspective.

As I take you along the journey of the Masteries, I will be asking you to often think in terms of themes, each of which contrasts the isolated, fearful state in which most of us live to the joyful state of peace. At the risk of being redundant, I'll suggest once again that you suspend your left-brain judgment as you read on. You'll find that the path on the road to freedom will, in time, reveal itself to you. Keeping that in mind, the following will serve as an introduction to the way we typically view ourselves in the world and a way in which we can see ourselves, and our world, as loving and gentle.

THE CONCEPT OF DOMINATION

I think you'll agree that our society is based on the concept of domination, in which we seem always to be in opposition to something. Domination requires that someone is better than you or inferior to you, that events or actions are right or wrong, and people are richer or poorer. It is almost impossible to feel safe or to relax when the world is your opponent. This paradigm pervades society and contaminates most of our thinking, leading us to a limited concept of reality.

Whenever you judge yourself or someone else, or you find yourself comparing yourself with others, or in some way measuring anything in your life against an external source, your thinking is based on domination. In domination we don't feel safe so we try to control the events in our lives, other people, or ourselves. Domination causes us to make our decisions based in fear. The best result we get when our decisions are based in fear is to generate more fear.

A society based on domination creates some very limiting beliefs about conformity and about shame. There is no room to embrace pain or limitations; you *must* overcome them; you *must* win. The very nature of domination requires us to struggle.

Living in a world founded on conflict, we feed ourselves a daily diet of insecurity. If you are honest with yourself, you'll admit that you sometimes compare yourself to others, or even the media version of who and what you *should* be. You are better than or less than; you do not have enough or are not successful enough; you are too fat or too thin. You feel pressured to conform. This type of thinking is very narrow and polarized. Domination can be symbolically represented as a line.

THE CONCEPT OF DOMINION

If, instead, we shift to a paradigm of dominion, our vision of life becomes expansive. In dominion, everyone is part of a greater whole; everyone is an equal and integral part of the circle of life. We are no longer residing in an either/or situation; the whole and the person become one. A person truly living in dominion cannot make a choice that will harm another. Rather than being fear-based, dominion is based in love, unconditional love for the self and all other beings great and small.

Within the context of dominion, the people in our lives become our assistants instead of opponents. The idea of competition no longer makes sense nor does it have any value. It is a totally different way of viewing the world, one in which peace of mind becomes a way of life. Viewed from this perspective, life becomes limitless. We can afford the "luxury" of treating everyone and everything with compassion, love, and equality. We are able to embrace everything in our lives because we no longer need to struggle against anything—we are accepting of who we are as we are. A person is honored for merely being alive; no one is ever judged. This kind of thinking is expansive. Dominion can be symbolically represented as a sphere.

We aren't trained to think in terms of dominion, so the concept seems frightening to many people. How do you live in a world based on domination and yet get your needs met if you remain in dominion? Won't people just walk all over you? Well, sure, perhaps some will. However, I believe that for the most part, we receive what we give. When we are loving and non-judgmental, we are treated in a loving, non-judgmental way.

Finally, when we perceive our lives as lived in dominion, the process of our personal transformation takes on a sense of gentleness and safety. As you work through the Toltec Masteries you will learn who you really are and to love that person unconditionally. This will be extremely difficult if you remain in a judgmental state of domination.

BEING AT FAULT

A concept that is related to the idea of living in domination is that of being at fault. Being at fault implies that either you or someone else did something wrong. If you perceive yourself as having done something wrong, or if you have the need to forgive yourself or someone else, you are contending with the concept of being at fault. Similarly, if you in any way feel the need to defend yourself, you are placing yourself in the position of being at fault, rather than being responsible.

When you're unsure of the distinction between being at fault and being responsible, and you are feeling at fault, you will ask yourself questions such as:

- Why does this always happen to me?
- How could I have been so stupid?
- How could they do this to me?
- What did I do wrong?

Perceiving yourself as being at fault is to perceive yourself as "stuck" and powerless. You judge yourself and others from a place of conflict. To grow, to change, you will want to begin perceiving yourself as responsible.

> **ASK YOURSELF**
>
> What do you hope to achieve by reading this book?
> How will you know if you have achieved it?

BEING RESPONSIBLE

The concept of being responsible is about your ability to choose how you respond to events in your life. Being responsible includes the ability to embrace an event, action, or emotion. We can't do anything wrong; we merely get outcomes or results we don't like. If we take responsibility for the outcome, we can lovingly explore the choices we made so we can make different ones in the future. If the outcome was "our fault," we will generally choose to berate ourselves for our choices.

In dominion there is no such thing as an error or mistake; there is merely an outcome. The word mistake takes on a new meaning; it means you merely need to adjust your choices so you will get a different outcome.

As you learn to view life from the paradigm of dominion it becomes much easier to take responsibility for the events in your life and to make different choices. Take some time to look at your definition of responsibility and make sure it is free of fault.

If you are taking responsibility, you ask yourself questions such as:

- What am I telling myself about this event?
- What could I have done differently?
- Why did I make that particular choice?

Does the idea of being responsible for your life or your experiences make you feel uncomfortable in any way? If it does, I guarantee that you have confused being responsible with being at fault. When you accept responsibility for your life it means you have the power to change. Being responsible for your choices is empowering and it is another one of the keys to achieving personal freedom

---

THINK ABOUT

What would you like your life to be like? How do you want to feel about the various aspects of your life?

How do you want to feel about:

- your work?
- your social life?
- your relationships?
- your spirituality?

Does your change and growth need to be a burden or something you really have to work at? How do you want to feel about your personal growth and spiritual explorations?

PERSONAL IMPORTANCE

Another aspect of living a life in domination is the concept of personal importance. When you are in personal importance you are always judging yourself and others. Your esteem comes from external sources and is very transitory. You aren't free to make choices; you are a victim of your thoughts and beliefs.

In a state of personal importance, you have no real power; you are disconnected from your essence and the universe. Any sense of power you have is an illusion. Personal importance tells you that you're right and others are wrong while it also tells you that you're wrong and others are right. Because personal importance is part of the illusion that we are separate, it lies.

As long as you are in personal importance, it is almost impossible to find a sense of peace. You are seeing the world as a place of struggle and divisiveness.

PERSONAL POWER

When you are operating from personal power, you are living from your heart or your spiritual center. You are making your choices consciously and making them based on love instead of fear.

Being in personal power, you view the universe from the perspective of dominion. You know you are part of that creative energy, part of the Creator, or as some people call it, God. Because you are connected to your source, you truly do have the power to effect change; you are part of the truth rather than the illusion. You know that you are responsible for the results of your decisions, and that you can use outcomes that you don't like as an opportunity to learn and grow. As you build your personal power, you increase your ability to access the divine and your vision of reality becomes clearer. You begin to see things as they truly are. Personal power and personal importance are inversely proportionate. The more you have of one, the less you have of the other.

FOLLOWING THE PATH

Attaining personal freedom is a process. Each of us has our own unique path; no two people live in the same world. We each live in a universe that is ours and ours alone. Finding your truth and accepting yourself and your universe is what this path is all about.

Although the Toltec tradition is filled with many wonderful tools, we can't really look to the past for today's answers. If any tradition had "the answer," we would already have "the solution." We wouldn't still be searching. But as we combine our own inner wisdom with the knowledge of the old ways, magic can happen.

This magic is the experience of our true nature. It is a new way of seeing the world based on unconditional love, dominion, and self-responsibility. It is the magic of engaging with the world from a position of personal freedom. Learning to experience our true nature is like learning a new language. If you learn the vocabulary of Spanish and use the grammar and sentence structure of English, your words won't make any sense. Don't try to fit this new belief system into your old one. If you do, you will find yourself becoming confused and frustrated.

Committing to Your Own Transformation

Think of your process as being as important as breathing. We never negotiate our need for air. We never put off our next breath until tomorrow. If we want to continue to live, breathing is non-negotiable. My guess is that Buddha, Lao Tse, and Jesus were all very well acquainted with discipline and dedication and the concept of making things non-negotiable. They said they were no different from us. Enlightenment is a state of mind; we could achieve that same sense of love, peace, and acceptance if we wanted to.

Do you want your life to be full of happiness and joy or pain and struggle? The choice is yours. And it all depends on how willing you are to exert the necessary discipline and dedication to change your old way of thinking. I mentioned earlier how I had to make certain tasks non-negotiable to keep me on my path. This deep level of commitment is critical to achieving a life that is a joy to live.

Your process is like a fitness program for your happiness quotient. If you want to get your body in shape, you'd probably join a gym. If you pay for your membership but never go to the gym, you won't see much progress. If you go every day but don't exercise, you still won't see any results. But if you go to the gym every day and increase your activity as your strength increases, before you know it you'll have the body you've always wanted. Of course, the right types of exercise and the length of time it takes to see results will vary for each person in the gym.

So it is with any process. If each day you spend a little time reading this book, doing some of the exercises, applying the principles, making different choices, and using the tools, before you know it you'll have the life you've always wanted. And of course, the experience will differ for each person.

One student explained the process in terms of sewing—when you want a seam to be very strong, you backstitch. You sew forward, then reverse, going back over the stitches, and then you go forward again making a much stronger seam. Our progress on this path is often a few steps forward then a few back before we begin moving forward again.

I see many of my clients struggle as they try to understand the concept of honoring their process. It is so easy to judge ourselves, or where we are in our process, or what is happening in our lives. But these assessments are counterproductive. Self-criticism only causes us emotional pain and makes us look away from the truth. Life can be a gentle process in which you remember who you really are, what is important to you, and what really matters. It is a process of going home, of finding your truths and your sacred center. My life changed drastically when instead of continually judging myself and constantly trying to find out what was wrong with me, I shifted the process to one of remembering—remembering how to love myself and stand in dominion with my world.

Acceptance, being gentle with ourselves, and telling ourselves the truth about where we are make learning about change much easier and more enjoyable.

This book is designed to make the process of loving yourself unconditionally as simple and as gentle as possible. A useful way to begin experiencing a feeling of self-acceptance is to do Meditation One in Appendix A.

Anyone can change his or her life, but you must remember that it is a process and that it takes time. Just as a flower blossom takes time to unfold, allow your process to unfold in its own way. So, be as gentle and patient with yourself as you would be with a flower bud. Take the risk of experiencing your true nature and allow yourself the gift of living within it on a daily basis. As the saying goes, "Even the longest journey begins with the first step." Join me in taking that step.

I'll explore the ways to do so through the Toltec Masteries in the upcoming chapters. As you read on, please trust that the concepts I've outlined above will have more meaning to you.

PART TWO

Awareness

Awareness is the first of the three Toltec Masteries and is the first stage on the path toward personal freedom. In exploring Awareness, the seeker might want to perceive herself as a student. To be a student you need only have an open mind and a great deal of curiosity.

If you would like to change yourself and the way you live, Awareness is a necessary ingredient. Awareness is something that continually deepens. As I release my limiting beliefs and assumptions, I become more and more aware of my true nature. Awareness allows me to see the world and myself as it really is rather than how I *think* it is.

As you explore the various aspects of Awareness, you will begin to understand your inner landscape and life in a completely different manner. As you increase your Awareness of how your life operates, you'll make different choices and you will be able to create what you want when you want it.

Sounds pretty good, doesn't it?

CHAPTER FOUR

The Illusion We Call Life

In a society based on domination, each of us must view ourselves as separate from, in opposition to, in competition with. From that perspective, we honor others' judgments of ourselves, rather than who we really are. In fact, because we are so busy evaluating ourselves in contrast with other people— their possessions, their "success"—we don't even know who we really are. How did we get here?

As children we aren't encouraged to follow our inner truths or to find our own voices. We are encouraged to conform and fit into society. We are seldom shown how to honor ourselves and are often judged for our uniqueness. We are trained by our parents and society to see the world in a certain limiting way and we accept those limiting beliefs as the truth.

> ### ASK YOURSELF
>
> What would your life be like if you could do anything, be anyone, and live anywhere?
>
> What would you do if you had all the money you could possibly want or need?

I call this barrier the filter system. Once we are trained we see through our filter systems instead of seeing the world as it truly is; it's like looking through a window covered with fog and raindrops—our vision is distorted. Eventually we see only our filter systems and don't really see life at all. (Bear in mind that our parents, our teachers, and the media train us to develop our narrow, limiting beliefs because to them, that is the truth—they are functioning directly out of their filter system and that's just the way life is.)

Living in our personal importance where we look outside of ourselves for meaning, we tend to focus on physical manifestations as the cause of our turmoil. We change jobs, relationships, and living situations only to find ourselves feeling the same way and having the same limitations reappearing in our lives. Because we bring our filter system with us to our new job, our new relationship, our new living situation, we naturally bring with us our limitations. I would argue that the cause of our turmoil is derived not from external events, but from our reactions to external events, determined by our filter systems.

THE AMAZING POWER OF YOUR FILTER SYSTEM

The Toltec knew that all of our limitations reside in our minds and are the result of our own choices. The way we think about events in our life determines our choices. How we think about things is the result of the beliefs, assumptions, and agreements we have about or with our world. We are not in touch with reality. What we are in touch with is our filter systems. This is how it works:

1. An event happens.
2. We observe it and attempt to understand it.
3. We have an emotional reaction to the event based on our limited understanding.

4. We generalize it, either making some assumptions about it, or relying on old assumptions.

5. Based on our assumptions, we make choices.

6. We make agreements with ourselves and the world about how we feel and how we will act in the future.

7. We now have a predetermined way of reacting to any similar situation.

Based on our experiences, we now *know* how to act. After that, the emotional response and the action are linked together, and we automatically react to a particular situation rather than choose how we want to act. Our filter systems tell us that is just the way life is: We no longer have to think; we project the past onto the present and react instead of choosing how to act. We see our filters rather than seeing life; it's safer that way.

ASK YOURSELF

What concepts in this book have you found unsettling or do you strongly disagree with? As you think about them, try to see your filter system, see if you can visualize any of your beliefs or assumptions that may conflict with the concept.

Why are assumptions so hard to release? Because our minds would rather be right than be happy. We are comfortable with our old assumptions, and we hold onto our limitations by arguing for them. I have seen people utterly locked into their personal perspective, although that perspective was causing them great emotional pain.

BREAKING THROUGH THE FILTER

Rightfully, you ask, so now what? You've been encouraged to create a filter system that confines your understanding of yourself and the world around you. You respond to events and other people on automatic pilot and you have no control over any of it. How, then, are you responsible for the choices that you make?

Stay with me. You can regain your ability to choose what you believe, how you are going to act, and what you want to feel. Start off by gently questioning your assumptions. Remember that an assumption is something that you think is true, but it is not something that you *know* is true.

Realizing that assumptions aren't facts, you are freer to make new choices and allow change to occur. As you read, notice your reactions, realize they are based on old assumptions, and for the time being, set them aside. See what happens. Simply notice when you find yourself disagreeing with the concepts being presented here or when you have an emotional reaction to the material. The stronger your reaction, the more attached you are to your belief or assumption. I have found that the more desperately I want to hold on to an assumption, the more freedom I have when I let it go.

TAKE TIME OUT AND ASK YOURSELF

For you, is the glass half empty or half full? What is your attitude toward life?

Notice how you think about love, intimacy, work, money, and play. Is it important to be busy? Do you need to have a partner?

What beliefs do your attitudes about life reflect? It is often hard for us to truly see our beliefs; after all, for us they are the truth. So relax and gently begin to explore your inner landscape.

How would your life change if you changed some of those beliefs?

A Simple Technique for Waking Up

The Toltec Mastery of Awareness demands that we wake up, but how do we do that?

The most powerful tool that you have for connecting with yourself is your breath. Early in my studies with don Miguel, one of the other students told me to pay attention to my breath. At the time, I thought little of his suggestion, but now I know what an incredible gift he was giving me.

You must breathe all the time or you die within moments, yet how conscious are you of your breathing? Right now, focus all of your attention on your breath. Really feel your breath. Feel the air as it enters your body. Where do you feel your breath and how does it feel? Is your breath easy or labored, hot or cold, moist or dry? Notice your chest and your shoulders. Fill your lungs slowly and completely. Now notice how you feel.

Generally, our first level of awareness is our thoughts. We hear our mind's endless chatter, below that are our emotions, and if we go a bit deeper, we become aware of what we are feeling in our body. In order to experience our true nature, we must be aware of what we are feeling. We must go beyond our mind and our emotions, and tap into our core, the essence of who and what we are.

71

Your breath can take you there. You have to breathe anyway, so why not harness it? I suggest you get a wristwatch with an alarm or carry a timer, and set it to go off every hour. When you hear it beep, focus on your breathing for a few minutes and ask yourself: What am I feeling? Then drop beyond your thoughts and emotions and feel the sensations in your body. Don't judge them or try to understand them; just feel them.

Once you are accustomed to monitoring your feelings, start asking yourself what you need at any given moment. Drop down below your thoughts and your emotional body's endless list of wants and needs and ask your inner self what you need. Then listen.

Whenever you think of it, notice your breath and drop down. Let each breath nurture you and fill you with love and awareness of your true nature. Your breath can be a very powerful tool, or it can be just your breath. The choice is yours.

As you practice following your breath to your inner self, you'll find that the way you think will begin to shift. You'll remember that the assumptions you have made about yourself and your world until now are all the product of your filter system. And you'll remember that the agreements you have made with yourself and your world about how you will feel and act are also the product of your filter system.

Once you remember you're looking through your filter system, you realize what you're seeing is not real and that you can change your response to it. Once you're able to do that you'll be able to experience whatever you want whenever you want. You will realize that you and you alone are the creative force in your life.

GO INSIDE

Take a few deep breaths and imagine yourself dropping down into yourself. With each breath, allow yourself to relax. Now picture yourself in the middle of a lake, calmly sitting on the surface. You are very comfortable and relaxed. Notice the surface of the water. If it is rough, simply calm it until the surface is crystal clear. Dip your hand in the water and let some drops of water run off your fingers. Watch the ripples go out from you as the water hits the surface of the lake.

Use this exercise to calm yourself and to get in touch with the core of your being.

73

TEACHING STORY

Using the Tools

The boy sat next to his father watching the wood chips fly. His father's hands were a blur as his tools moved over the log. The beak of a huge bird was taking shape before his very eyes. The wings were magnificent, so crisp and clean you could see each tiny feather.

He watched his father's face as he wiped his brow and took a long, deep drink of the cold spring water he had just brought him. The man's eyes never wavered; he gazed lovingly at the wood.

"What do you see, Father?"

His father seemed startled by his voice. His eyes then focused on the boy and he smiled.

"Look here, my son, and you will see the spirit of the wood. In order to create these great totems, I must first become one with the wood. Tools alone won't set the images free.

"Look at the grain of the wood, see how it moves throughout the wood. Feel it, let the wood speak to you. You must let it tell you what to do next.

"For me to make the next cut I must be gentle, I must barely cut the surface or the beak will crack. Can you feel it?"

The boy held his tiny hand on the log for a long time. His father watched in silence. Finally the boy nodded.

"I feel a tiny river of energy flowing though my hand. It tickles. If I push down too hard it stops."

The father smiled and nodded to his son. He picked up the knife and began to carve again.

"Tools are important. I must care for my chisels, keep them sharp and free of rust. I must learn what my tools can do, how to use them, and how to care for them. But my most important tool is my heart where my spirit resides. My heart will always tell me what tool to use and how to use it. My heart will tell me when to push forward and when to go slowly. My mind cannot guide me; it sees an image and forgets to listen. Then the wood breaks and I must start all over.

"Learn to listen to your heart. Listen when your heart tells you about life. Listen when it tells you to let go or move on. Listen when it tells you it is time to stand your ground or when it is time to go beyond your mind's fear and change. Your mind will run from change, it will run from fear and in the running lead you into greater fear. Learn to listen to your heart my son, it is the most important tool you will ever have."

"How do I learn to hear with my heart Father? So often my mind fools me, I think I am listening to my spirit only to find it is my mind filling me with its lies."

"First you must learn how to listen, my son. Listen to the wind, feel the rain, walk in the woods, and ask nature to teach you. Practice humility, practice saying "I don't know." Your mind always knows the answer, it always knows what's right and what's wrong, and it always has an opinion. Your heart is a quiet, gentle whisper. It will remind you of your perfection and talk to you in the language of love. Your mind is much more like a crow, loud, bold, and raucous. It will remind you of your limitations and why you can't do something. Its language is fear. Learn to feel the difference. Your mind will usually lie and say, "Of course you're listening to your heart." Just as it took me time to learn how to use this chisel, learning to listen to your heart will be a wonderful journey. Discipline and dedication along with the sincere desire to listen to your spirit will set you free, but it will take time and practice."

The boy stayed and watched as the images in the wood took shape.

CHAPTER FIVE

Creating Clarity

To attain Awareness is to see with clarity. See with clarity? What does that actually mean? To me, to see with clarity involves eliminating our filter systems from our world view. This is no simple task. To truly see yourself and the world with a new set of eyes you must be open-minded; you must be teachable. In the beginning of this section, I suggested that the reader consider himself a student for the purpose of attaining Awareness. I'd like to revisit that idea now and then turn to how we unravel our filter systems.

BECOMING TEACHABLE

An attentive, eager student will be honest with himself about what he does and does not understand. One of the first steps in achieving Awareness is developing the ability to tell ourselves the truth about where we are right now. Once we tell ourselves the truth, once we have an empty cup and say, "I don't know," we become teachable.

An American businessman went to a famous Zen master. He wanted enlightenment. He sat down in the chair and waited very impatiently, tapping his feet and looking at his watch. The master finally walked in and offered him a cup of tea. The man took the cup and looked at the old man very critically. He wanted wisdom, not tea. The master started to pour the tea, and he poured, and he poured, and he poured. The cup overflowed, spilling tea all over the man. The man jumped up very angrily.

"What's the matter with you, old man?" He yelled.

The master smiled and said, "It is impossible to fill a cup that is already full. Your mind is already full. Only an empty mind can be taught."

What does this story tell us about Awareness? To be aware, we need to take a hard look at our assumptions. When I realized that my assumptions were one of my greatest obstacles, I started to question them. As long as I held on to my assumptions, I wasn't teachable. In order to make changes, I had to have an empty cup. When my assumption is unassailable, I *know* I'm right. I have the answer and I am no longer teachable. In order to *see* the world differently, I must be *willing* to see it differently. And so, join me with an empty, open mind as you examine how you see the real world, rather than the one created through your filter system.

THE UNIVERSE YOU CREATE

In the previous chapter, I stated that our filter systems distort our perception of reality. There really is no "out there." The external universe acts like a huge mirror accurately reflecting your filter system. The external universe is an energy system based on action and reaction. We have a thought or a belief, we seemingly interact with someone or something, and then we react to their reaction.

On the other hand, of course, there's a world out there populated by billions of other creatures. Events happen beyond our control and we have to make choices about what to do next. Lovers come and go, we find jobs and lose them, we move, we have children, parents and friends die, and life goes on. Our lives are filled with dramas that involve any number of people.

Many of us devote great energy rehashing what we believe has happened to us:

- "If my mother had taught me how to love myself, I would be able to be assertive."
- "If only they treated me better, I'd be happier."
- "If I only had more money, or more time, or a nicer place to live, life would be better."

We all have a story we call our life and the truth is there is no one else out there; it is all our projection.

But of course people do things, events happen, and there are unsafe places to live. Life is easier when we have more than enough money to pay our bills, and when we are treated with love and respect by the people in our lives. The paradox is that if you want to achieve personal freedom, you must fully accept the idea that "out there" is merely a reflection of what is going on inside of you.

Yes, we do have an impact on others and the world has the ability to have an impact us. Physical reality exists but if we want to grow, if we really want to be free of our limitations, we must ignore those facts for the time being. We must play a game in which we have no doubt that there is absolutely no "out there" and that we are playing in a room of mirrors that gently and accurately reflect our filter systems. If there is no "out there," we can take full responsibility for all of the experiences in our lives. And remember—being responsible is simply the willingness to accept the outcome of our decisions. It is our ability to change our response. It has nothing to do with being at fault.

Looking Inward

All that is "out there" is your own projection. Looking within yourself for all your answers will be the hardest thing you ever do. It will also be the most rewarding. Don't kid yourself—accepting the fact that there is no "out there" and taking full responsibility for all of your emotional pain and limitations is an incredibly courageous act. Your bravery will be rewarded—I guarantee it.

During the course of my studies I learned to view physical reality as a complex energy system that was part of me, that I was a part of and to which I contributed. As I began to see the universe as an energy system my world became a very accurate, non-judgmental mirror of myself. As I dropped some of my own personal judgments and limitations I realized that everything happening in my external world accurately mirrored how I felt about myself, the beliefs I held about myself, and the assumptions I had about the world as a whole. At first I tried to ignore what I was seeing; I tried to change things externally—as if they were not a reflection of myself—but it didn't work. The harder I tried to fix the external aspects of my world, the more fleeting my happiness became. Eventually I realized that if I didn't like what I saw "out there," I did have the power to change myself, my inner world, my beliefs, and my perspective. I realized that if I didn't like what I was seeing in the mirror I had to change myself, not the image I saw in the mirror.

Ironically, as long as I wasn't trying to change "out there," as long as I was really focusing on changing myself, "out there" changed. The paradox is that if I want to change "out there" I can't. Life mirrors our inner world; change that and the image in the mirror changes too. I began to ask myself questions like, "What set of beliefs does this situation suggest?" "What am I telling myself about these events and the choices available to me?" Eventually I was able to lovingly and gently ask myself the question, "What choices would a person who loves herself unconditionally make in this situation?" Inevitably the question changed into, "What new choices do I need to make if I want a different outcome?"

I embraced the concept of life as a process in which I make a choice, observe the outcome, and then make another choice. The first step in the process was learning to ask myself questions and then being able to hear the answers.

The Words You Speak to Yourself

A subtle way that we keep our filters intact and distract ourselves with the *mitote* of our minds is through our internal dialog. Do you consciously listen to your internal dialog? Do you know what you tell yourself that makes you feel angry, sad, or happy? Today your mind said 95 percent of the same things it said yesterday; they were limiting thoughts then, and they still are today. Becoming aware of your internal dialog takes practice. Your habitual inner dialog constantly reaffirms your filter system and it stops you from being able to heal your emotional wounds. Once you become aware of your inner dialog you can change it to a gentle, nurturing, encouraging voice supporting you in your quest for personal freedom.

Listen to what you say to yourself on a regular basis. Start selecting what statements you choose to believe or listen to. Ask yourself if there is a more expansive way of speaking to yourself.

MONITOR YOUR INTERNAL DIALOG

What do you say to yourself about:

- yourself?
- your abilities?
- your future?
- your body?
- your home?
- the events in your life?
- your friends?
- life in general?

Mirror Work—An excellent way to start is by talking to yourself in the mirror. You can begin by looking deeply into your eyes, taking a few deep breaths, and taking a few minutes to really look at yourself in the mirror. You might feel silly looking in the mirror and talking out loud to yourself. But who cares? You're talking to yourself all the time anyway. So go ahead. Take a few minutes to connect with yourself. Then begin saying things such as: I love and accept myself just the way I am. I deserve to be happy, joyous, and prosperous. Life is easy. I am safe and I can choose to be happy no matter what is going on around me.

Often when you say these kinds of things to yourself, your mind will respond with a variety of statements that I call "yeah buts." "Yeah, but I am not good enough;" "yeah, but life is hard;" "yeah, but. . . ." Your mind has an endless list of yeah buts; they consist of your limiting and toxic beliefs. As you become aware of those statements, it is important to remind yourself that they are just opinions; they are not facts. When you become aware of any limiting beliefs, acknowledge the old thoughts, tell yourself they aren't true, and remind yourself of the new thoughts you are trying to integrate.

START WORKING IN THE MIRROR

Make a commitment to do mirror work twice a day. Look deeply into your eyes and say:

I love and accept myself just the way I am.
Life is limitless. All is well in my world.
I deserve to be happy, joyous, and abundant.

Keep reminding yourself of your new truths. Create your own positive affirmations and see what happens. When you want to change your inner dialog, first say something like, "I used to believe 'A' and I know that is false; I now choose to believe 'B'." Every time the old thought arises, counter it. In time, your thoughts will change.

Always use statements that are positively phrased because your mind doesn't tend to register negatives. If you say "I don't want to be angry," your mind hears "be angry." State what you want to experience instead of restating what you want to change, or what you don't want.

One of my clients felt depressed, so I suggested he do some mirror work. He went home that week and very diligently wrote down all the statements he said to himself. He returned with pages and pages of negative comments about his self-worth, his abilities, and his experiences. Not surprisingly, he was still quite depressed. I complimented him on completing the first step by becoming aware of his self-talk. Then I explained that the next step was reminding himself that his inner dialog wasn't accurate. He needed to change the dialog and start telling himself the truth. I reminded him to counter the negative comments with positive statements. The following week he reported feeling much better.

Working in the mirror is a powerful, transformative tool. I recommend doing it at least twice a day. After working with the mirror for a while you will become more aware of your inner dialog. It will become second nature to monitor it and, when necessary, to remind yourself of the truth. As you begin paying attention to what you are telling yourself, you will become aware of how various statements make you feel.

WHAT DO YOU SAY TO YOURSELF IN ORDER TO FEEL

- happy?
- sad?
- angry?
- worried?
- excited?

- pensive?
- tired?
- stressed?
- loved?
- loving?

How Easily We Fool Ourselves—When I was teaching inmates in the local correctional facility about self-esteem I would talk to them about the correlation between their inner dialog and how they felt about themselves. They seemed quite skeptical when I told them that what they said to themselves mentally affected them physically. To demonstrate, I would have one person stand in front of the room with his arm extended straight out in front of him. I would tell him to resist as I pulled down on his arm. Then I would tell the inmate to make these statements out loud: I am a wimp. I have no physical strength. I am a weakling. I am a failure. Amid much laughter he would humor me; after a few seconds I would pull on his arm, and it would go down quite easily.

After I demonstrated with several inmates they began to see how their internal dialog affected their lives. Begin to notice what you say to yourself. As you begin noticing

89

your internal dialog it may be uncomfortable; you may find yourself feeling worse for a short time. You always talk to yourself but may not have been consciously aware that the conversation wasn't based on the facts.

As long as the conversation remains subliminal it is much more damaging. When we become conscious of the dialog, we have the opportunity to change it. You can choose to continue saying the same things to yourself or begin talking to yourself in a more loving manner. Make sure you take the time to counter all of the negative statements with positive, gentle, and loving statements.

The Words You Speak to Others

If we are not actively conscious of the words we say to ourselves, our internal dialog and our filter system will work hand in hand to reinforce one another. Similarly, our communications with others are contaminated by our filters and our filters keep our communications in check. Our communications are not composed of just the words we speak, but of the relative value that we place on them as well as on the amount and type of power we imbue them with.

By using many different "channels," we can put a variety of energies behind our words. The different channels are just like those of a radio or television, and we can choose the one we want to get a particular response. We can use our voices to create love and harmony or fear and control.

Communication is a very complex matter. Think of the phrase, "What do you want?" These four very simple words can take on a whole host of meanings depending upon your tone of voice, your facial expression, and the energy you put behind them. Those simple words could convey love, judgment, compassion, disgust, anger, or deep caring. Those few short words can convey anything from "how can I help you" to "get out of my life." And how would you really know the difference? The person speaking the words could mean one thing while the person listening to the words might hear something entirely different.

Until we learn how to consciously choose what channel we are going to use, our filter systems choose for us and we will continue to get the same responses. Change the channel and the responses will change.

We all know what it feels like when we are judged by someone else, even if they never speak judgmental words. Behind the spoken word lies a more accurate channel of communication, of which we are often unconscious. We may innocently say to a friend "you look nice today" while at some level we are still upset with her about something she said several days earlier. On the channel we use, we communicate our annoyance and our friend is left guessing, do we dislike her outfit or her? Once we bring all channels of communication into conscious awareness we can clearly communicate exactly what we want to communicate. It does require quite a bit of courage, because for all levels of our being to match we have to be rigorously honest and vulnerable.

How does your voice sound when you're afraid? What kind of words do you choose to use? Now think of the way

OBSERVE YOUR COMMUNICATIONS FOR A WEEK

Do you ever stop yourself from saying something? If you do, why do you stop yourself? Do you ever say something and then regret saying it?

What are your habitual channels of communication? Practice using different channels when you communicate. How often do you use the channel of love? Experiment with what happens when you put the energy of love behind your words.

How often do you use the channel of fear? Notice what happens when you put the energy of fear behind your words.

you feel and speak when you feel safe, honored, and loved. What is the difference? If we learn how to use the channel of love we can speak out on issues and get a loving response in return. The next time you speak, ask yourself what channel you are using. Experiment with the energy you place behind your words. Notice what happens when you speak in anger, love, fear, or with distrust or honesty. The world is a very accurate mirror. See what happens when you change the energy behind your words.

It should come as no surprise that without an awareness of your filter system's role in your communications, you will not be able to tune in to the channels of love and acceptance. Just as with your inner dialog, you must be consciously aware of your outer dialog if you want to change it.

Managing Our Emotions

We believe that other people or external events are "causing" our emotions, but in fact, we create our emotions by what we tell ourselves about the events in our lives. That is not to say that we shouldn't acknowledge our emotions. Most of us have spent years ignoring them, judging them, or having other people discount them. Your emotions are your emotions; they aren't good or bad, or right or wrong. They just are. Your

93

emotions, however, are not facts. They are more like valuable clues telling you about your beliefs and internal self-talk. We tend to think our emotions are real and that they are based on external events. They aren't. Ultimately, how we feel is our choice. External events don't make us feel anything.

When you make statements like "you hurt my feelings" and "you make me so angry," you are not telling yourself the truth. The truth is that the person did something and then you told yourself something about his actions, which generated your emotions. It would be more accurate to say: "When you did 'A,' I said 'B' to myself and now I feel 'C'." In order to get to that perspective you will have to change some of your beliefs and take responsibility for what you are telling yourself about the events in your life. Be gentle with yourself as you begin moving in that direction.

Achieving any degree of emotional neutrality is incredibly empowering. You are no longer a victim; your peace of mind and happiness are no longer dependent on other people or events beyond your control. You can decide how you feel regardless of the events in your life.

All of our emotional responses are based on our personal perspectives and they are totally subjective. As you move toward an attitude of emotional neutrality, you also move toward a greater degree of personal freedom. It is much easier to see what choice would be most beneficial when you aren't overwhelmed by your emotions.

It takes time and practice to become emotionally neutral. You can begin by noticing what you are telling yourself. If you are angry about something, start by admitting that you're telling yourself that event is making you angry. As much as possible, detach from the event and go inside yourself so you can become aware of your inner dialog.

We are strongly invested in our emotions. Be patient with yourself—becoming emotionally neutral is a process. It is hard to admit that our emotions are self-generated; we don't really want to let "them" off the hook. If you are angry, fearful, sad, hopeless, or joyous for that matter, it is because you are telling yourself something. Emotions are all based on judgments. Release the judgments and your emotions will change. You can practice placing yourself in a non-judgmental state by doing Meditation Two in Appendix A.

ASK YOURSELF

What are your favorite emotions?

What emotions do you avoid?

The Toltecs recognized that we create our own emotions—they are not truly a response to something or someone else. Because each of us is the source of our emotions,
we need not, indeed, should not, take anything personally.
When someone loves me, she feels that way because I awakened her own self love. I don't take it personally. When
someone dislikes me, it's because I've awakened the pain of
her own self-judgment. Regardless of her emotions, they are
not about me; they are about her inner world.

What does all this have to do with seeing with clarity?
When we see with clarity, we are aware of reality, rather than
the universe we create with our filter systems. We're accustomed to having an emotional reaction to events "out there"
that is essentially pre-programmed. When we recognize that
"out there" is of our own making, we can consciously choose
how we want to act. And when we recognize that all the
people in our lives see the world through their own filter system and are acting accordingly, we need not waste another
moment concerning ourselves with their judgments of us.

At this stage in your process you will find it very useful
to differentiate between your emotions and your feelings. We
use words like anger, sadness, joy, or happiness to describe
our emotions. Emotions are always caused by our filter

systems. Feelings are physical sensations you experience in your body and emotions do cause feelings in our bodies.

It takes a great deal of practice to stop reacting to events in your life. Start by asking yourself frequently throughout the day, "What am I feeling?" Begin to separate your emotions from your feelings. I suggest carrying a small notebook and writing down your feelings and your emotions. It is also a good way to stop yourself from reacting. Start by noting what you are feeling in your body. Notice if your chest is tight, if your shoulders are relaxed or full of tension. Rapidly scan your body and note the sensations you feel. Then move on to your emotions, what names would you put on them? It takes time to become aware of your feelings and not automatically translate them into an emotional response.

As you get in touch with your emotions and feelings, your natural reaction will be to blame them on something "out there." Try as hard as you can to stay neutral. Remind yourself you are merely feeling the energy; it is neither right nor wrong, neither good nor bad. It is just your body's reaction to events happening around you. Eventually, as you get in touch with the energy, you will intuitively know what actions are necessary to regain your inner balance and create the outcomes you desire.

PERMITTING YOURSELF TO BE AWARE

There is something within us that allows us to be aware. It allows us to be aware of our existence, of our thoughts, of the people around us, and of the world in which we live. Our ability to focus that awareness, our ability to see things differently, is one of the keys to our personal freedom. That energy within us that allows us to be aware is totally loving, absolutely limitless, free, and non-judgmental. As we learn to align ourselves with that energy, everything changes for us.

For a moment, imagine a child without a care in the world—one that feels cared for, safe, loved, and totally accepted. Now imagine that child running around in a vast amusement park where there are no waiting lines, entrance

WHAT AWARENESS MOST AFFECTS YOUR LIFE?

- the awareness of fear of intimacy
- the awareness of the effect of your filter system
- the awareness that you are not your mind
- the awareness that you create all of your emotions
- the awareness that there is no "out there"
- the awareness that there is no need to judge anything, especially yourself and your feelings

fees, or height requirements. There are lots of friends to play with, the weather is perfect, and there are no limits to how much fun that child can have. Just imagine how you would feel if you were that child. You would be able to be in the moment, free from your limiting filter system. You could follow the energy wherever it took you without endless self-doubts. Life really is a vast amusement park designed to assist you in remembering your divinity. Take time to enjoy it.

TEACHING STORY

Words and Wounds

The evening wind began its journey just as darkness fell. The moon was a thin sliver in the eastern sky. Off in the distance the coyote's plaintive call echoed throughout the canyon. She had to keep moving; there was no time for rest. She must get to the top of the cliff before the others. The girl had promised herself time and time again to stop gossiping; she had sworn she would never make this mistake again. But she had, and now she had to save face or be banished forever.

Even the evening breezes couldn't keep her cool. Sweat poured off her body as she neared the top of the cliff. She almost fell because her wet hands kept slipping off the rocks. She crawled over the top; her chest heaved as she gasped for breath. She ducked behind a rock and hid. She looked around carefully and it looked like there was no one there. She was relieved she'd made it.

She leaned back against the rock and relaxed. Out of the darkness she heard a voice. She sat perfectly still, listening and hoping. But then the voice spoke again.

"Come here, my child, you can't hide from me."

Her shoulders started shaking and she wept; she'd failed to get away. It was the Grandmother.

"Come, my child, you have nothing to fear."

Slowly she walked toward the voice. The Grandmother stepped out of the shadows and motioned for her to sit on a nearby boulder. The girl sat down and hung her head in shame. The Grandmother knew the girl had been telling stories again.

"I am so sorry, Grandmother. I swore I would never gossip again but . . ."

Grandmother held up her hand and motioned for her to be silent.

"Sit and listen. The village knew before the words left your mouth, my child. Everyone knows your heart, they know your pain, they know, little one, they know. It is time to forgive; unless you do you are doomed to wander the desert without a home. You will die alone with your pain. Only your pain will go with you."

"But, Grandmother, I . . ."

The Grandmother rose and as she stood before the girl, her eyes filled with rage.

"Go no further with your stories. Be quiet or I will withdraw my protection. Many in the village want you gone because of the pain you have caused with the vicious gossip you spread. It serves them to believe your gossip so they can hurt each other. It must stop. You must stop, you must heal your pain and learn to walk in love."

An old man stepped out of the shadows. It was the girl's uncle. At the sight of him, the girl's body filled with anger and she lunged at him with all her might. But she fell in the darkness and found herself on the ground. She turned and he was still standing there. She expected him to be laughing but instead there was a tear rolling down his cheek.

"I hurt you, my child. I did unthinkable things to you; I tormented you and taught you to hate. I am sorry, I was wrong. I forgot about gentleness and love, I used my power to control and hurt others. I wounded your heart and taught you to see only from your wound. Let it stop here.

"No one believed you when you went to them with the truth. They made fun of you and believed your stories were childish lies. For that I am truly sorry. You have paid a heavy price for my torment. But there is still time for you to change. Let Grandmother help you, let me help you, learn to walk in love and let go of your fear."

The girl's eyes stung as tears of anger and sadness streamed down her cheeks. Grandmother held her gently and hummed a song of love and healing.

"Child, in order for you to heal, you must want to change more than you want to stay the same. You must realize there is a problem before you speak, not afterwards when you are afraid of being caught. Once a word leaves your lips it is too late, you can never call it back. You must change that which causes you to act. You must heal the wounded parts of your spirit so they too are filled with love instead of fear.

"Just as the hunter tracks his prey you must track your mind. You must find the places fear lives and fill them with love. You must understand what you decided as a young girl, how you were going to make sense of the pain. You must change what you came to believe about life and about others. Then gossip will no longer be necessary. You will be free. You need never forget but you must forgive. Do this for yourself; as long as you hold onto your anger your uncle's cruelty cannot die. Learn love from your uncle's betrayal instead of perpetuating the hate."

"But, Grandmother, how will I ever be able to fill a hole that has no end? My pain is too great."

"It only seems that way, little one. Every time you speak of your pain you open the wound and deepen it. Make a different choice and let the love in. When you want to cry out, tell yourself the truth. You're afraid, you gossip to cover up your fear. The truth will set you free.

"Now go, child, go to the place of your ancestors. Sit in silence until the truth is revealed to you. Pray and ask for help. Ask for the willingness to see the truth. When you are done come to me. I will know your heart and with my help you will learn to walk in love.

"Go in peace. All will be well, my child, as long as you remember your old ways serve you not. Your healing always lies in the opposite direction your mind tells you to go, so learn to listen to your spirit. Your spirit will set you free.

"You must learn to connect with your spirit and your heart. Your spirit must become the master of your mind. Your mind is a wonderful tool but a very poor master. Now go in love."

PART THREE

Transformation

Transformation is the second of the Toltec Masteries, and it corresponds to the stage of development referred to in the Toltec tradition as being a hunter. A hunter learns the habits and routines of his prey so he can successfully capture it. In your tracking exercises, your personal history will serve as your prey. You will be seeking the events, the assumptions, and the beliefs that you've developed over your life. When you capture them, you can evaluate how they have affected you and how you can choose to transform them. You can then release them.

In a way, the Masteries of Awareness and Transformation are quite similar. In the former, you learn that your emotions and your actions are "automatic" responses to the beliefs that you've created through your filter system. You learn that your filter system prevents you from seeing reality and that it acts as your "interpreter" of what is external to you. Finally, you learn that what is external, what is "out there," cannot be changed. What can be changed is your perception of it and your response to it.

In the process of Transformation, you will use the tools of recapitulation, tracking, and writing your Book of Freedom to assist you in looking at your past in a new light. Through tracking, we develop an awareness of what triggers our behaviors. As we explore the triggers we begin to realize what we have to gain, and what we have to lose by changing the behavior. Once we thoroughly understand the reasons for our old choices we can begin to make new ones.

We all have a history. When we meet someone, we have a story that we tell called "our life." Our story is full of facts, events, emotions, and happenings. It is a myth. This myth is based on our beliefs, agreements, and assumptions; as a creation of our filter system, it is highly distorted. By clearing out my filter system, I've been able to transform my childhood.

When my first book *Dance of Power* was released, my father asked me how I could tell all those lies about our family. I hadn't cleared out portions of my filters yet and I shared stories about my childhood as I remembered them. When I asked my dad about his recollection of those stories, his versions were entirely different. He remembered them through his filter system as well. Neither of us was accurate. Now I remember those events differently. I know that my filters still color them; but the filters are a bit clearer and more loving.

We take our story so seriously. We often defend our right to be miserable by refusing to change the story. For years my favorite role was playing the victim. I was very skilled at the role and could turn even the most good-natured person into a victimizer. Until I was willing to let go of that story line I made very little progress in my emotional healing or spiritual explorations. I had a hard time letting it go because the person I victimized the most was myself.

I felt comfortable in the role of victim; I did "poor me" so well. It was familiar, safe, and comfortable. At first, I had no idea how it would feel or how to act if I stepped into my personal power and let go of my personal importance. I terrorized myself and made the process so much harder than it had to be. Once I accepted that I was comfortable with it and that playing that role had served me, I could start to change.

There are still times in my life when I can feel that old role welling up inside of me just wanting to come out. I can still do a pretty good whine—but I don't take it very seriously for very long. And, if I feel a need to play "victim" for a while that's fine, because I can change how I feel anytime I choose.

As soon as I stopped judging myself I could engage my sense of humor. I could lovingly laugh at myself and move on. I find it far easier to change when I'm amused by my behavior than when I'm judging it.

Our beliefs, the roles we play, our filter system, are all just part of a story we remember to tell ourselves every morning and all day long. Your life is based on your mythology. If you're willing to change your mythology your life will change drastically. Change is only as difficult as our attachment to our story makes it.

You already know what your personal myth is, and you can rewrite it from scratch. What would you like it to be instead?

CHAPTER SIX

Recapitulation

In the tale about the Zen master, I mentioned that we have to have an empty cup, a completely open mind, in order to be teachable. Your personal history is like a cup that is over-flowing with events, assumptions, and agreements that you've made with yourself about how to respond to the world. When you track yourself, you examine your past and let go of it so that your cup can be refilled.

Recapitulation is a simple breathing technique that allows you to release the past on an energy level. Every piece of information in your mind has an emotional component and an action component. Almost every memory you have has some kind of an emotional charge attached to it. If you were bitten by a dog as a child, chances are you are afraid of dogs. Although lovable to others, dogs might terrify you because of your past experience.

The stronger the emotional component, the more rigid your thinking is around a particular issue.

Recapitulation allows you to release the emotional component so you can "see" an issue more clearly and make different choices in your life. We are free to choose based on what we want to create rather than on what we believe about the past. When a doctor hits your knee with that little hammer your leg automatically swings, and when you hit one of your emotionally charged memories you automatically repeat the same actions. Until we release the emotional charge or the energy behind our decisions, making new decisions is very difficult.

THE TECHNIQUE

The actual process of recapitulation consists of two types of breaths: the inhalation and the exhalation. They are two entirely different types of breaths that are practiced separately.

These breaths are designed to remove any emotional charge or energy you have attached to old, stored memories. It is important to keep the energy aspect of the two breaths separate. When you are removing energy from the event don't give it back with the same breath. When you sit down to recapitulate I suggest you practice doing it for at least fifteen minutes at a time.

I like to begin the process with a short opening prayer. If you want to, take a few really deep breaths, relax, and say something like this:

Opening Prayer

May this place be made a sacred healing space. May all that I release be transmuted into love. May I have the willingness, courage, and strength to see what I need to see with clarity, compassion, and understanding. May that which most serves me come to the surface of my consciousness so I may heal the past and live in love always. I give thanks.

The Inhalation Breath

The inhalation breath focuses on taking back any energy you have given to a person or event. In order for us to be upset by someone or something we have to give it permission to upset us. In a sense we have to give away a piece of ourselves. With the inhalation breath we take back that piece of ourselves, that energy, that we have devoted to the person or event. The Hawaiians believe we leave behind little energy filaments wherever we go. We leave behind a part of our energy unless we choose to take it back. The ancient Hawaiians would periodically cut the filaments so they could regain their *mana* or spirit.

Obviously with each breath you inhale and exhale, but here you focus your attention on the inhalation. As you inhale you imagine yourself pulling energy in like you are sucking on a straw. Inhale through your mouth. It helps if you simultaneously sweep your head. Start by looking over your left shoulder and slowly inhale as you move your head to the right. Finish inhaling as you reach your right shoulder. Then exhale as you move your head back toward your left shoulder, putting no emphasis on your exhale. You are merely releasing the air in your lungs. Inhale through your mouth and exhale through your nose. Let yourself really feel the energy filling you as you inhale. The energy is now yours to use as you like. It is no longer connected in any way with the occurrence or person that was troubling you.

The Exhalation Breath

The exhalation breath gives back the energy we received during a particular event or exchange. For example, if someone was yelling at us we give back their anger, shame, or judgment. They gave us a piece of themselves and we return that piece to them.

The exhalation breath focuses on releasing any energy you have attached to a memory. As you exhale, imagine yourself blowing out energy like you would a candle. Start by looking over your right shoulder and exhale, pushing out the energy as you slowly move your head toward your left shoulder. Finish exhaling when you reach your left shoulder and inhale as you move your head toward the right. Place no emphasis on your inhale, just fill your lungs with air. Exhale through your mouth and inhale through your nose.

When through with a recapitulation session, you might want to say a closing prayer. Before the prayer take a few normal, deep breaths, and allow yourself to be fully present in the room.

Closing Prayer

I give thanks for the healing that has taken place here this day. In the coming days may the understanding of these events be revealed in a gentle and loving manner. May I be an instrument of love and peace in this world, now and always. Help me to fill my heart with love, compassion, and understanding. As I go forth from this place help me to be free of fear and help me to love myself and others unconditionally. Thank you.

RECAPITULATING YOUR LIFE

Recapitulate your entire life? Am I serious? Well, yes, I am. The rewards for doing so are countless, and all you need is a little organization. If you want to recapitulate your entire life, you need to make a series of lists. Often our mind feels so overwhelmed at the prospect of making these lists that we never get started on the process. If you start the lists and add people and places to them as you think of them, you'll be surprised at how fast they get done.

I suggest making five lists. Make a list of all the places you have ever lived, of all your romantic partners, of all the other people you have known, of all the jobs you've had, and of all of your pets. Of course, if you've never had a pet, you can eliminate a list right off the top.

WRITE STORIES

Write your personal myth as it is now. What is the story of your life? What is the logical outcome of your myth? Are you going to live happily ever after or are you the tragic hero or the nasty villain?

Write a myth of your life from the perspective of personal power. Ask yourself what really matters to you and create a life based on it. Let your imagination soar as you write this myth of your possible future.

I found that if I started with the places I lived I could fill in the other lists much more easily. If you can't remember a person's name, just write "the store clerk" or "Joe's friend." All that matters is that you know the person to whom you're referring. Then design a system for yourself. I find it easier to start with a house and bring in the events and people I remember from the time I lived there.

Some people choose to start with a theme, such as relationships or a specific feeling. For example, if you frequently feel victimized, you may want to start with that feeling. Feel free to focus on whatever feeling is most prevalent in your life. Then start with the most recent event that elicited that feeling and work backward in time until you reach the first time you felt that way. Allow the process to be organic but just make sure you are systematic enough to cross everything off your list. Whatever works for you is what works for you.

Depending upon the issue, you either start with exhalation or inhalation breaths. If you are very upset with a person I suggest starting with exhalation breaths. It doesn't really matter which type of breath you do first, you just do it until you feel like you don't have anything to give or take back anymore. Then you do the other breath until you feel as though you have completed that one. Always use both types of breaths on each issue you recapitulate during an individual session.

If an issue is particularly emotionally charged it may take several recapitulation sessions to clear it. I know I am done with an event or series of events when I have what I call a moment of clarity. I see clearly how my filters created the events and I am able to view them with no judgment whatsoever. Then I know I am done. It takes as long as it takes to really release an issue, so allow yourself to repeat the process as often as you need.

Set aside a time once a day or once a week to recapitulate. I start out by saying a short prayer and then breathe for fifteen minutes. I say a prayer of thanks and give myself a few minutes to write or think about what transpired during the session. Strong emotions at times are normal; at other times I've felt numb. There is no right or wrong way of doing this as long as you do it.

HAVE A CEREMONY

Spend some time alone in a place where you feel connected to your source. Create a ceremony of forgiveness and forgive yourself and anyone else you feel needs forgiving.

RECAPITULATION IN THE MOMENT

Recapitulation can take on many forms. You can practice it daily, releasing the stored energy from the past and taking back energy that you've spent. You may like to devote each session to a particular person or feeling.

With practice you can do it in the moment when you are feeling yourself hooking emotionally and recapitulate an event as it occurs. For example, imagine that you had an argument with a coworker. You sit down and start breathing. If you really allow yourself to complete the process, you will not only feel better but you will see your filter system as the cause of the reaction you had and be able to act differently the next time.

Once you become really proficient with the process you can do it in the moment. While you are talking to someone you can breathe the situation in and out so you don't feel compelled to react. If a person is yelling at you, rather than take on his anger you can breathe that energy out. If you find yourself emotionally hooked you can take back that part of yourself by breathing in. It just takes practice and a bit of discipline and dedication to remain emotionally neutral.

THE POWER OF RECAPITULATION

By recapitulating my life I literally created a different childhood. When I was young I felt constantly judged by my mother; I felt unloved, alone, and abused. I spent years doing inner child work and trying to heal my "abusive childhood." Then I recapitulated my past. Once I did that I could see very clearly that my mother was saying "I love you" yet I was hearing "there is something wrong with you" because of my filters. I could see how even as a child I was creating my experience of reality with my filter system.

Now as I look back on my childhood I can see my mother's perplexed face. I remember her saying "I am just trying to help you." She was saying, "I love you" the only way she knew how, yet I couldn't hear it when she said it that way. I imagine she couldn't hear "I love you" the way I said it either. We came together to learn how to say "I love you" and we missed the mark. Recapitulation can set you free from your filters, or at least allow you to see them more clearly. I hated giving up my mother as my scapegoat but I eventually had to if I wanted to be happy and free.

REVIEW YOUR JOURNEY

Thus far, what have you found most valuable in this book?

Recapitulation will assist you in emptying your cup so that you can fill it with new versions of your memories. If you take the time to thoroughly recapitulate your life, you'll find yourself with boundless energy to create yourself anew.

CHAPTER SEVEN

Tracking

The Toltec Mastery of Transformation helps us to view our personal histories clearly and to reshape them so that we can act as we choose, rather than react to old triggers. One method of releasing our past is known as tracking.

Tracking isn't a purely intellectual pursuit. When we track an issue we don't try to figure it out with our mind. We allow ourselves to drop down into our emotional core and feel. When we are connected to our feelings we can sense intuitively what an issue is about. Our feeling nature has nothing to do with words and it differs from our emotions. It is closely related to our connection with our spiritual self.

As with all the techniques on the path to enlightenment, tracking requires curiosity and open-mindedness. Before you track an issue, you'll want to ask yourself some questions about it, perhaps write about it and think about its symbolism for you. These first steps are necessary and very helpful, but the real work begins when we start looking at the issue from an energy level.

THE TECHNIQUE OF TRACKING

Start by setting aside an hour or so. After you become more proficient (and you have fewer issues to track), it might not take as long, but for the first few sessions make sure you give yourself enough time. Find a place you'll be comfortable. You'll want to write about what you discover after the session so make sure you have paper and a pen. In the past, I might have had profound insights and was absolutely certain I would never forget them, so I didn't write them down. Nonetheless, a few minutes or hours later I couldn't remember them no matter how hard I tried. So write down your insights.

Take a few deep breaths and relax. It is time to go inside to see what you are feeling. Some people envision getting very small and sinking down into themselves, others ride in a magic submarine, and others imagine themselves inside a cave deep in their heart. Visualize any situation that works for you. Imagine yourself in touch with your inner self. Identify an issue that troubles you, such as difficulties you are having with your boss, or why you purchase things that you don't need. Now gently bring the issue into your conscious awareness.

Take a few more deep breaths and ask yourself what the issue is *really* about. Get quiet and listen. Breathe in love and exhale anything unlike love. As you view the issue, notice what you are feeling in your body. Use your bodily sensations as a bridge. Follow them into the deep recesses of your filter system and listen. Listen to your feelings, let yourself know, hear what you tell yourself.

Think of the issue as a thread. As you pull it up you find a variety of thoughts and feelings attached to it. See what is attached to this issue in your mind. Follow it wherever it leads you.

Then take a few deep breaths; avoid trying to analyze the problem intellectually. Just let the thoughts and

127

feelings come to you. Relax and allow yourself to feel your connection to your spiritual self. Remind yourself that you don't know the origins of this issue, and ask to know what the issue really is. Reminding yourself "you don't know" is an important part of the process. It will allow you to see beyond your filter system to the truth.

You may have to do this process several times before you are clear about the issue. After you relax and drop down into your emotional self, take a few minutes to write about the issue. Don't direct your writing; just let it flow. This will allow you to get more clarity. Repeat the process as often as possible until you have that sense of relief, that inner knowing that you just "got it." And remember that even after you got "it" there is more "it" to uncover.

Logically assessing the issue or understanding it rationally is not what you want; they are actually the booby prize. Understanding the issue in the traditional sense is really just another way of "seeing" through your filter system. Successfully tracking an issue generates a deep feeling; it is an understanding at a core level that goes beyond words. I most easily describe it as a profound feeling of relief that you finally know what your problem is really all about.

THE POWER OF TRACKING

Tracking an issue can help you make great strides in resolving it. For example, suppose that you are tracking your inability to have successful relationships. At first glance it looks like your relationship problems are created by the people that you choose. If you learn to choose different types of people, your relationships will be successful. That may be true, but the people you choose are consistent with your beliefs, your assumptions, and your agreements, so you need to go deeper.

The people in your life are a reflection of your filter system. So to see your filters you must look at the pattern. What type of people do you choose? Are they angry or fearful? How do they treat you? Do they mirror how you treat yourself, or do they mirror some old belief? Keep asking yourself questions about them and remember the answers are not about them—they are helping you define your filters. The answers to your questions about them will help you track your thought patterns and elicit your emotional wounds.

Often, we can easily see when a friend is repeating his old patterns and making the same choices over and over again. We might even see the belief he has that causes him to make those choices. Although we are adept at understanding our friend, it is much harder for us to be equally objective about ourselves.

And so, when you look at yourself, try to be as objective as you would be if you were thinking about your friend. If the people you choose are angry, ask yourself if you're angry. If you aren't, ask yourself what they represent. Is anger familiar? Is that how your parents treated each other? Is that a reflection of your definition of love? Without judgment, explore what the people you choose represent symbolically in your life.

Once you understand what role the people you choose play, go on to the next level. Explore your inner definitions of relationship itself. How do you think a relationship should look? There will be several levels to your answer. There will be the level of what you consciously believe. You might think that relationships are supposed to be loving and free of conflict. Then there's the level of your filter system. Perhaps at that level you believe that relationships never work, that people will always leave you, and that relationships only cause pain. You might find it helpful to visualize your filter system just melting away, so that you can develop a new set of beliefs. To assist you in this process, try Meditation Three in Appendix A.

Tracking is a process of going deeper and deeper into your filter system until you "see" what the real issue is.

ASK YOUR DEEPEST SELF

What would you most like to change about your life right now? Use this issue to practice tracking.

Take some time to observe yourself in relation to this issue. Carry around a notebook and write down as many details as possible about it. Include how you were feeling, what was happening, and what you did. Try to notice your internal dialog.

Set aside an hour to track the issue. Go into a light meditative state and drop down into your feelings. Follow your feelings and see where they take you. Give yourself time to see the beliefs and expectations you have surrounding this issue. Write as much as possible about the issue until you sense that you're done.

When you've finished, take some time to write about your insights.

Did you find the process easy, confusing, or difficult? Write about how this process feels to you. Do you find yourself resisting it in any way? What way could you view this process that would assist you in "seeing" your filters more clearly? What could you tell yourself after a session that would be most beneficial?

When I tracked relationships I found that my problems had nothing to do with relationships at all. At some level I believed life was meant to be hard and that the best I deserved was to suffer. I thoroughly believed that if I got too happy, sadness was sure to follow. I believed that when something good happened it was always followed by something bad.

Obviously, I didn't deserve to have good relationships, so I could see to it that they were not a part of my life.

Tracking takes patience and practice. This process is like peeling an onion—there are many layers and you have to go through them one layer at a time. Relax and allow the process to unfold gently. Allow for the possibility that it is a skill you can develop and use successfully. If at first, you have tracked an issue and you find that your choices don't change, dig a little deeper; they will.

If you combine tracking with recapitulation, the results are amazing. You can use recapitulation to assist you in getting emotionally neutral so tracking will be easier. When you drop down into your feelings, use inhalation and exhalation breaths to remove any emotional charge so you can see the issue clearly. Remember that this is not an intellectual process and that you are not to focus on external events.

The focus should be on what you are bringing to your issues so that you can release your past assumptions and agreements. You can then make new decisions about how you will act in the future.

TEACHING STORY

The Vision Quest

The girl wandered the woods all day with anger driving her and sadness filling her heart. She too wanted to go on a vision quest, even if they were only for boys. Now that the sun had set, she felt fear dancing at the edge of her consciousness. She was lost, her stomach was empty, and she was thirsty.

She sat quietly by a tree and listened. The wind had always guided her, but her anger had drowned out its voice. The leaves began gently moving so she stopped to listen. She followed the wind. The air was fresh and sweet with the smell of water. After a few moments she found herself standing beside a brook. She thanked the wind and dipped her hand into the cool water to quench her thirst. As she looked up she saw a young fawn watching her. Their eyes met briefly before he ran off to join his mother.

She crossed the stream and filled her stomach with ripe berries and pine nuts. Summer was almost over and the earth was bountiful. It was too late to try to find her way home, so she wandered along a path until she came to a beautiful clearing. The moonlight filled the area with a shimmering light.

She raced into the center of the clearing and began to sing and dance. Ecstasy filled her young body and she danced until she fell to the ground exhausted. She drifted into a deep sleep but the voices kept calling her back to consciousness. Finally she pulled herself awake.

When she opened her eyes the world looked very different. When she tried to move her feet she found she couldn't. Then she looked down at her body and screamed. Her young body was covered by gnarled old bark, her arms had become limbs, and her feet went far down into the earth. She was a tree, an old gnarled tree.

"What happened to me? What have you done to my body?"

Laughter filled the air.

"I don't find this at all funny, now give me back my body!"

"Not so fast, my child, take time, watch, and listen. You will learn much," said the wind.

The young girl took the wind's advice and began to calm down. She listened in silence and watched intently. As she looked within her new body she felt only acceptance, love, and a great deal of patience. There was no need to hurry; the seasons would come and go no matter what she did. In her branches she supported many families; there were birds, a young squirrel, and colonies of ants. The wind constantly caressed her and the earth met all her needs. She was at peace and one with all about her. She sighed and surrendered to the feelings of peace filling her heart.

She had a great deal of knowledge but she had no idea where it came from. The voices were quieter now but she could still hear them if she listened carefully.

"Who are you?" asked the young girl.

"We are the ancestors, my child. We are the keepers of the ancient mysteries. We store all the knowledge of the earth for all time."

"Where are you?"

"We are all around you, my child."

The young girl grew silent and in that moment she knew. "You are the trees that speak to me, aren't you?"

"Yes, my child, we are. We have stood silently bearing witness to all that has passed upon this earth. Our roots go deep and spread across all the land. We have long been the keepers of the knowledge. In times gone by, beings of your kind knew that and honored us. They would come to us in times of trouble to ask for advice. They would come to us in times of joy to share their happiness. They would bless our spirits for warming their homes and cooking their food.

"Some of the tree spirits would speak to your people though their carvings. We stood as great totems before their villages and held the spirits of their nations, but your kind has forgotten. You think we are just trees. You forget that you owe your very lives to us. We make the air you breathe and guide the winds upon the earth so the rains come and the air stays cool. We are glad you finally came to us, child. We are grateful one of your kind is once again willing to listen."

The young girl felt the sap coursing through her veins and knew the truth of the words she had just heard. The trees saw all and knew all. They understood with love so they held the knowledge in a clean and pure light. A tree embraces the moment of transformation with joy—man calls that moment death and fears it.

The young girl was lost in her new world and her spirit rejoiced. The last thing she heard was a voice telling her, "Teach others how to talk to us, teach others to know our love. Share the gift you have been given."

When she awoke she was lying in the clearing looking up at the stars. She stretched her arms and realized she had returned to her old body. She immediately felt sad but then she heard the murmuring of the voices. She raced over to the nearest tree and threw her arms around it. She opened her heart and she was one with the tree. She would never see life in the same way again.

The next morning she had no trouble finding her way home; the trees guided her. Her mother was filled with both anger and relief when she saw her daughter walk into the village. She was about to admonish her daughter, when she saw her eyes. They had changed; they were no longer the eyes of her young girl. Her daughter was filled with wisdom far beyond her years.

The mother silently led the girl into the center of the village. The girl sat at the edge of the well and waited. Slowly, one by one, the villagers started to gather. She told her people of her vision. She picked up a piece of wood and gave thanks to the tree that had agreed to become fuel for their fire, to warm them, and cook their food.

She led the little ones over to the nearest tree and taught them how to listen. She told them to stand with their backs against the tree and ask for its wisdom. Next they needed to take a few deep breaths and call upon the four directions and the four elements. Then they were to stand in silence and let the energy of the tree flow through them. After a few moments, if they had truly surrendered, they would feel a gentle rocking. When the rocking eased, they could merge with the tree and see the world through its eyes. She reminded them to always give thanks and to approach the tree with humility and in love.

She took the elders over to the oldest tree at the edge of the village. She said a blessing and introduced them to the spirit of the tree. For years the men had gathered here to talk and confer; now they knew why. They offered thanks. There was much laughter and joy as they sat down to commune with the spirit of their new friend.

As she fell asleep that night the young girl looked up at the branches that held up her roof and gave thanks. She prayed that some day humans would learn to take time and talk to the trees. She smiled, for she knew she would meet the spirit of the trees in her dreams. She would remind all who cared to listen of the gift trees had to offer.

CHAPTER EIGHT

The Book of Freedom

T he mind wants to be right; most of the time it would rather be right than be happy. Robert Bolton once said, "A belief is not merely an idea the mind possesses; it is an idea that possesses the mind." If you want to experience personal freedom you must break free of your mind, you must end the war between your mind and your self, and lovingly take control of your thinking. You must set your spirit free and become who and what you've always been.

Writing your Book of Freedom will help you do just that. My teacher, don Miguel, never taught in absolutes.

He would make suggestions and whether you followed them would be your choice. When he introduced a process similar to this to his students, he told them they either had to do it or they could no longer study with him. That was how important he thought it was.

Writing your Book of Freedom is an arduous process but the rewards are immeasurable. Most of my students resist because they don't like to write, or they don't have the time, or . . . the excuses go on and on and are sometimes very creative. The question I pose to you is this: In five years you'll be five years older and if you don't actively do something to change yourself, your life will be pretty much the same. If you really use this tool you'll be five years older and your life will be totally transformed. Imagine it's five years from now, which choice do you wish you'd made?

Remember what I said about making steps in your process non-negotiable? Writing your Book of Freedom should be non-negotiable, just do it, and see what happens. I guarantee your life will be transformed. If you are diligent and follow all of the directions as written, you will learn to see life through the eyes of love and fear will leave you.

THE BOOK OF FREEDOM—OVERVIEW

This journaling process has several different components. There are sections you write in daily; there is another section you work on throughout the day, as well as sections you write in periodically to release the past or re-create the present. It is a very easy process if you stay in the moment and don't overwhelm yourself. Just read through the directions and follow them step-by-step. If you have a great deal of resistance to the process, track your resistance. This book is your ticket to personal freedom.

Your mind is meant to be a tool but it has learned over the years to chatter endlessly. This incessant noise is the *mitote* of the mind. Your mind can learn to be quiet and only talk when it's necessary. I leave my computer on all day. When I am not actively using it I have the screen saver set so the screen goes blank. When I want to use my computer I touch a key and it's ready and willing to serve me. It doesn't sit on my desk and endlessly talk to me. It doesn't demand my attention or offer me its personal opinions. It just sits there and waits for me to use it. Your mind is a wonderful bio-computer. The Book of Freedom will allow you to turn on the screen saver option.

In all, you will need to keep three separate journals. The entire process will take about an hour a day and may take over a year to complete. Once you become accustomed to the process and your mind starts to quiet, the amount of time you devote to it daily will decrease.

The first journal can be in the form of a small book, or a small tape recorder, that you carry with you at all times. In this book you will record your mind's meaningless chatter. When I did this it was amazing how fast my mind stopped talking; it didn't want to have to record all those thoughts.

In a second journal you will write twice a day, at morning and at night. You can use one journal as long as you have separate sections for each function. I remember spending days finding just the right journal and pen. It was a wonderful excuse not to begin. I suggest you just grab some paper and get started; actually the present is the only time you can change anything. So get your pens ready!

The largest journal, the Book of Freedom, is broken down into two parts, the Book of the Past and the Book of Creation. In the Book of the Past there are five sections, the biography, the section listing all your beliefs, the section dedicated to final judgment, the section devoted to the voice of the victim, and a section to break free of personal importance entitled "I'm sorry, you were right, and I was wrong." The Book of Creation is not divided into sections. It contains your thoughts on living in a state of love. This journal will take time to complete. I suggest setting aside at least an hour every week to work on this journal.

The writing is specifically designed to help you re-train your mind. You may find all this writing annoying and that's great. The annoyance will create the momentum necessary for you to stop thinking the way you have been.

On the first page of all my journals I have a contract with myself that I sign and date. I read it every time I open my book. Sometimes I read it when I don't want to write and it reminds me of why I undertook this process in the first place. I suggest you read the copy of my contract below and then use it to design your own.

"I, _____, agree to write only the truth, as I now know it, in these pages. I have decided to follow this process so I may free myself from the limitations of my mind. I promise myself that everything in this book will be as honest as possible. My intention in writing in this book is to

145

create the internal need, a sense of clarity, and desire to relearn and select all the knowledge, assumptions, and beliefs I choose to store in my mind. I will use this book to re-train my mind and learn how to choose when I think and what I think about. I dedicate myself to the process of this Book of Freedom. I ask for help and assistance as I take on this formidable task. I ask for the willingness, the openness, and the courage necessary to stick with the process. May this process help me see myself and my world through the eyes of love, compassion, and forgiveness. May I always remember that this is a process of healing and remembering. I promise to be gentle and loving with myself as I proceed with this process."

Signed _____

Dated _____

146

Write a similar contract in your journal. Use your own words and emphasize what's most important to you. This would be a good time to create your definition of personal freedom. Incorporate it into your contract. Make this a contract of dedication to your personal freedom.

Give yourself the gift of doing whatever it takes to achieve a life filled with joy.

JUST DO IT

Are you finding reasons to put off starting your Book of Freedom?

Explore your resistance to the process, but start your Book anyway.

Chatter Book

During the day you need to carry a small book or tape recorder with you. Every time you have a judgment about yourself or someone else, you need to write it down or record it. Every time you have a thought that isn't loving or powerful you record it. If you think like a victim, act like one, or feel like one, write it down or record whatever you were thinking or saying to yourself.

On a moment by moment basis you are going to record everything you say to yourself every day that is judgmental and unloving. Remember, today you thought 95 percent of the same thoughts you thought yesterday. If you are diligent about this part of the process, you can diminish this tedious repetition. You can begin to speak to yourself in a more loving and supportive manner. You can also change what you think day after day. When your mind was being programmed for you as a child, you never had the opportunity to choose what thoughts were being put into it. Now you do. This process will give you the opportunity to consciously choose what you are thinking rather than listen to an endless series of thought loops repeating themselves.

Daily Journal

Every morning and every night, set aside a few minutes to write in your journal. In the morning sit down and write two or three pages. Write whatever comes to mind. As your mind thinks, write down what it says. Don't censor anything or try thinking about a topic—just write. I find I need to write at least three pages because it takes a page and a half or so for my mind to let go of the pen.

After the first page or two I'm able to let out whatever words I need to write. You write these pages before you do anything, before your first cigarette, before you shower, before you fully wake up. Get out of bed, quickly go to the bathroom, then just sit down, and write. You write whenever you first get up; if you work nights write when you wake up in the afternoon. If you meditate in the morning make sure you write first.

I highly recommend writing a minimum of three pages. On some days I write more but I always write at least three 8½ x 11 pages. Some people use a time limit but I find a page limit works much better for me.

In the evening, spend ten or fifteen minutes reviewing your day. Notice if there were any themes or recurring thoughts and see if you need to take any actions the next day. If you are worried about something, write it down and turn it over to your spiritual self. Then write a list of all the things about your life and yourself that you're grateful about. List at least ten things daily and try to add a few more each day. Really fill yourself with a deep sense of gratitude and love before you go to sleep.

Spend a few moments focusing on the progress you're making. Focus on creating a feeling of gratitude that you're in the process of freeing yourself from being a slave to a mind filled with fear. As you fall asleep, re-dedicate yourself to loving and accepting yourself and to awakening to your divinity. Fall asleep surrounded by a feeling of love, acceptance, and peace as often as possible.

The Book of Freedom, Part 1: The Book of the Past

This journal is divided into five sections: biography, beliefs, final judgment, voice of the victim, and "I'm sorry, you were right, and I was wrong." Its purpose is to break up or free you from your personal importance. Your personal importance will probably get insulted, have resistance to the process, and try to stop you from doing it. Your mind will suggest shortcuts that I can guarantee won't work; it will tell you to skip this step and come up with hundreds of reasons not to do it. Your mind may want to turn to the next chapter. But your Book of Freedom is your connection to your spiritual self.

Your Biography—In the biography you write the story of your life. If someone picks up your book and reads this section they should know all about you and the significant events in your life.

Your Beliefs—You will work on this section for quite some time. Set aside time each week, think about what you believe, and then write your beliefs down. As you notice beliefs, add them to the list. Your beliefs will come in many shapes and forms. You might believe rainy days make you feel sad or that if something good happens it is always followed by something bad. They might be in the form of stereotypes, such as redheads have bad tempers. Every time you become aware of a belief write it down.

Final Judgment—In this section you write down all the judgments you have about yourself, other people, society, and life as a whole. The reason the section is called final judgment is that your intention in writing down your judgments is to release them. The end result of this whole process is to see life through the eyes of love. Love is always free of judgment and as a result of this process you will stop judging anything or anyone. This section, in combination with the writing you do during the day, will train your mind to stop judging.

When you observe yourself judging something avoid judging yourself for judging it. Observing yourself from a neutral prospective is much more useful. If you do judge yourself, write it down or record it.

The Voice of the Victim—In the victim section, write down all the thoughts you have that are victim-like in nature. Just listen for the voice of the victim or martyr and write it down. As you write down these statements, do it with the intention of letting the roles go. The role of the victim is one of the most common roles we play in our lives. We are the creative force in our lives, yet we constantly feel victimized by events in our lives; people upset us, and society and the world are frightening places. As things arise during the day, record them. Allow yourself to become aware of how the voice of the victim operates in your life. As we think so we are. If we learn to think powerful, loving, and supportive thoughts, we needn't play the victim anymore.

After you are finished with this part of the process you can proceed to the next step. This first part of the process will take at least several months if you are very dedicated. It may take a year or more if you're not. Don't move on to the next section until you have completed those mentioned above.

IMAGINE

What if you viewed your unwanted qualities as gifts? How would that change your life? For example, what if you thought of your nervousness as excitement, or your judgment as discernment? How would you change your unwanted qualities into gifts?

I'm Sorry, You Were Right, and I Was Wrong—This section is the hardest of them all. Your personal importance will fight doing it. It is also the most freeing. This step will remove any false sense of self. It is important that you do this step with a deep sense of self-love and not because you have to. Some of the concepts are challenging, but they are very freeing.

Do not even attempt this section until you have *completely* finished the other sections. Once you have released a large portion of your filter system, writing this section makes a great deal of sense and is very liberating. Until then, most people find themselves getting very angry at the idea. I have had people storm out of class enraged when I raise this topic, especially people who have been abused as children or lost loved ones at the hands of another.

Life as we perceive it is not real. If you've really released the voice of the judge and the victim, this process is the next logical step. If you find yourself defending yourself and trying to make the other person wrong, remember that your filter system is at work. Don't try to proceed; redouble your effort on the other sections until you feel comfortable moving forward.

Forgiveness and acceptance are something we do for ourselves and not for anyone else. If we are unwilling to forgive someone we're only hurting ourselves. The need to forgive arises from our judgments. As we release our judgments, we naturally move towards acceptance. We aren't now and we never have been a victim to anyone or anything. That may seem like a harsh way to view life if we've been physically or sexually abused. But life is just a story we tell ourselves; the events are merely shadows caused by our filter systems.

Sometimes we create rather dramatic events in our lives just to divert our attention. Our life is like a movie. If a movie has a strong spiritual message for us and in some way awakens our divinity, should we ignore the message and get caught up in the story line? Should we forget to accept the gift of our awakening and get bogged down in what happened to one of the characters? We frequently do that in our lives. We forget that we are just characters. We get caught up in the story and forget we are really spiritual beings having human experiences on the stage of life.

Everything in our lives is there by invitation. We don't consciously invite it in, but it is the logical outcome based on the beliefs in our filter systems. Until I recapitulated my childhood I felt I had been badly abused and felt very unloved most of my life. Once I saw my filter system, I could see how my reactions and my filter system caused me to feel that way. My mother could have been Mother Teresa and I still would have felt unloved.

A DIFFERENT KIND OF MIRROR WORK
Find a gentle path somewhere out in nature. Take a small hand mirror and walk around backward looking into the mirror for guidance for half an hour or so. Notice what the world looks like in the mirror. Write about what your mind has to say about the experience. Then feel how your spirit responds to it.

Some boys sexually abused me as a child. Once I saw my filter system, I could see the fear in the faces of my attackers; I could see they were trying to change how they felt inside by controlling and manipulating me. We did a cosmic dance together. I needed to let go of my old way of seeing the event if I wanted to be free. They were taking actions that were consistent with their filter systems and so, in their minds, they didn't do anything wrong.

No matter what happened in your past, you're the one who's still suffering by holding onto your memory of it.

155

We'd rather be right than happy. When you get to the point that you can say to someone, no matter what they've done, "you're right, I'm wrong, I'm sorry," you're free. You no longer have any judgments or attachment to the event and you are no longer affected by it. If you've been abused, molested, or "hurt" by someone, don't you want to be free of the event? Would you like to turn back the clock so the event never happened in the first place? Well, this is the next best thing.

The reason we say "I'm sorry, you were right, and I was wrong" is to free ourselves from the judgments we've had about the person or event. Those particular words and the concepts behind them are used because our personal importance hates to say it was wrong, and this exercise is designed to assist you in smashing your personal importance. Right and wrong are part of the domain of our filter systems so we use them to help set ourselves free. After all, according to the other person's filter system, he was right. Who are we to question his filter system? He was right; his mind told him so.

Once again, do not attempt this part of the Book of Freedom before you are really ready for it. After you have released your internal judge and victim, make a list of all the people in your life who you have ever offended or hurt in some way. Now add the names of all the people who you feel have hurt or offended you.

The list is easy. The next step will take time, willingness, and dedication. In some way, either personally, by phone, or in a letter, contact everyone on your list. In your own words very clearly communicate that you're sorry, they were right, and you were wrong. Don't go into long explanations or in any way dilute the message. Do not defend yourself or judge them in any fashion.

If you can't find the person, or if she has passed away, write her a letter anyway. I often burn the letter or mail it with no return address. Just make sure you release the contents of the letter so you can finally move on. As long as we think that we're right and they're wrong, we're the ones who are trapped.

For some of the people on your list you might have to write, scream, yell, recapitulate, and then do it over again until you can really get emotionally neutral about them. And that is the gift; you get to let go of all that trapped energy. In the process you will get to see your filter system and release its grip. You will be free of your limited thinking and be able to see that person through the eyes of love and compassion.

Start out by making the list. Don't worry about the second part. Dedicate yourself to your personal freedom, take a deep breath, and begin. You're worth it.

> ### SELF-TREAT
> Make a list of behaviors that feel loving and nurturing to you. Do at least one every day.

The Book of Freedom Part 2: The Book of Creation

This final section of the journal is dedicated to love, light, and laughter. You could call it the book of life; it is a journal where you focus on becoming a servant of love instead of a slave to fear.

You have looked at how you compromised your personal integrity in the previous sections; now you are going to concentrate on how you maintain it. I define integrity as our sense of wholeness. Our integrity grows and changes as we do. What was acceptable a year ago may no longer be acceptable. But ultimately our integrity allows us to become whole or one with our spiritual self. Anything that stops us from experiencing our own godlike nature is an assault to our personal integrity. Our thoughts, beliefs, actions, assumptions, and anything that prevents us from knowing ourselves as divine causes us to compromise our integrity.

In this section explore your personal code of conduct. How do you want to act? What is important to you? What choices do you make if you want to remain loving at all times? Are there still behaviors and thought patterns that cause you to compromise your integrity?

Also ask yourself what you want in your life. Dream. Go out and look for places where you feel your wholeness. There is no longer any excuse not to be happy. If you find an excuse, let it go. How are you going to make yourself happy? How are you going to be of service to love in your life instead of being a slave to fear?

Write about all the issues and limitations you discovered in the other sections. How are you going to think about those things now? How are you going to define love, abundance, relationship, and joy? Systematically address each of your old limitations and find a new way of looking at them. Set your thinking and yourself free.

This process will be organic. Your thinking will constantly become freer and more expansive. You will begin to understand the meaning of unconditional love and acceptance.

At times you may have to cycle back into the other sections and explore issues at a deeper level. I find that my mind gets very noisy whenever another issue is rising to the surface of my consciousness. I don't judge or resist it; I just embrace it and use my tools to explore it. The Book of Freedom will be with you for the rest of your life. Sometimes I don't need mine for months but when I do it is always there. I can pick it up and use it whenever I need to.

Relax and allow for the possibility that you can and will do it. Be gentle with yourself and as loving as possible. If you have resistance to the process, love even your resistance. Love it and let it go; then do the writing anyway. Give yourself the gift of freedom.

PART FOUR

Intent

Intent is the third of the Toltec Masteries. It corresponds to the stage of development in the Toltec tradition referred to as being a warrior. As a warrior you are practicing the skills of emotional neutrality and awareness so you can choose more clearly when and how to act. You are close to achieving personal freedom so your choices are based on your connection to your spiritual self rather than your filter system.

Our Intent directs our energy and dictates the form our creations will take. It is a very powerful force in our lives, yet we are often unaware of it. We have allowed the energy of Intent to become enslaved by our filter systems.

Intent works either consciously or unconsciously, but it is always operating in our lives. Once you learn how to consciously harness the power of Intent, anything is possible. Intent works hand in hand with the other two Masteries. If you set your Intent to be aware of your filter system, you will stop focusing on the "out there." If you aren't actively conscious of your Intent, chances are your Intent is to defend your filter system and your limitations, so you will.

Our lives constantly reflect our Intent. If you look at the results you are getting in your life you can understand what your Intent has been. If you are unhappy, your Intent was to be unhappy. If you say your Intent is to quit smoking and you continue to smoke, then your Intent was to continue smoking. By using your ability to track yourself and see deeply within, you can understand your motives and use them to change your Intent.

Intent and the will complement one another. Think about a sailboat with the wind blowing strongly in its sails. The Intent is the wind, and the will is the rudder guiding the boat. Your will directs the energy that propels you forward. Your Intent is part of the divine force that allows you to create your experiences in this life. Focusing your Intent with your will allows you to become a co-creator with God.

Intent is often hard to see directly but its reflection in our lives is always crystal clear. In order to thoroughly understand Intent, we will have to approach it from several different directions. Be gentle with yourself, embrace your outcomes, and Intent will become your greatest tool. Judge yourself and your process and you can be certain your Intent is to stay the same, not change. In the following chapters, I'll explore how to discover your Intent and how your life will change when you align with the Intent of your spiritual self.

CHAPTER NINE

Discovering Your Intent

If you have worked at the Toltec Masteries of Awareness and Tracking, you've learned that the things that "happen to you" are of your own creation. You've also learned that although focusing on what is "out there" doesn't serve you, you can change yourself, and in the process "out there" may or may not change. By acknowledging your filter system, you see that you have developed a set of assumptions, beliefs, and agreements that have served to control your behavior. By tracking yourself, you've found that you can release the unwanted energy you've stored in your personal history and take back the energy that you've devoted to retaining painful parts of your past.

When you focus on your intent, you can truly begin to act as the creative force in your life.

Intent is a very powerful energy. It has a very distinct feeling in your body. Being in alignment with your intent feels very different from listening to your filter system.

Asking yourself, "what do I want to create right now?" will help you to refocus your Intent. If your answer is, "I want to feel safe," what you really want to do is defend your filter system. Whenever you are feeling the need to be safe, fear is present. Fear is only present when you are listening to your filter system. If you are focusing on what could have been or should have been, instead of what is, you're stopping yourself from being able to create what you really want right now.

Once you're aware of your Intent you can change it, and the only way you can change anything is to change what you're telling yourself and by modifying your behaviors in the moment. Moment by moment you must focus your attention on what you want to create and avoid focusing your attention on what you don't want. If I say to you, "No matter what you do, do not, I repeat, do not think about a red fire truck," you immediately think about a red fire truck, don't you? Your mind and the universe don't hear the negatives. Your mind has to think about a red fire truck in order to not think about it. By focusing your attention on what you don't want, the energy of your Intent is wasted.

You have undoubtedly heard of the power of positive thinking. Thinking positively, thinking about what you do want to create, is fruitful. For example, if you think to yourself, I want to spend this afternoon feeling peaceful and happy, you can in fact spend it feeling peaceful and happy. On the other hand, if you think to yourself, I don't want to be miserable anymore, or I don't want to be broke anymore—guess what? You'll create misery and lack of money. Your words and thoughts are very powerful, so make sure you choose them well.

Your life always accurately mirrors your Intent. Once you recognize your Intent, you can change it moment by moment by changing where you focus your attention. For example, if you notice your intention has been to move away from pain you can change that. You can decide to move toward pleasure instead. As soon as you hear yourself saying things like "I don't like that" or "I don't want that," you can focus on what you do like or what you want instead. As soon as you notice your old behavior you can say, "I'm sorry" to yourself or someone else, forgive yourself, and then make a new choice with love.

THE SOURCE OF YOUR INTENT

A good way to change your Intent is to ask yourself if your current choices are coming from personal importance or personal power. The two feel very different. When your Intent is in alignment with your spirit, your choices will be coming from personal power. When your Intent is coming from personal importance, you can be sure you are defending your old worldview; your filter system has you by the tail and it is running the show. Your Intent is always visible in your life. Whatever you are experiencing, whatever you have created, has been created by your Intent.

Another way to examine your Intent is to check your list of favorite emotions. We are frequently attached to certain emotional states; for example, we are actually comfortable feeling angry with ourselves or at others, and we defend our right to feel that way. Our Intent is to feel that way so we create situations that give us a perfect excuse to feel that emotion.

One of my students worked with me for several years learning and growing, but she was unable to change some of her core behaviors. One day as we were tracking her process, she realized her intention had been to hurt herself and cause herself a great deal of disappointment. She realized she was most comfortable with that feeling; it was safer and less risky than feeling happy or content. As long as that was her Intent, change was impossible, and she consistently made choices that would cause her pain. Once she changed her Intent, her life changed rapidly.

ASK YOURSELF

What do I want to create right now? Whenever you find yourself feeling fearful or worrying, ask yourself again what you want to create; then take an action consistent with that desire. Try asking the question every half hour for several days.

CHAPTER TEN

Surrendering to Your Intent

Intent can be likened to faith. When a person has a profound faith in God, he easily believes everything that happens in God's world is for a purpose and there is an inherent order to the universe. He thinks in terms of divine order and in God's time. If you place your faith in Intent, if you allow yourself to have total faith in your Intent, miracles will occur in your life. Surrender to your Intent; it is what's creating your experiences in life anyway so why not learn to harness that energy in a positive manner? Stop fighting, stop defending the Intent of your small self and harness the energy of your spirit. Align yourself to the Intent of your spiritual self.

In this context, surrender means letting go so you can harness the energy of your divinity. It is hard to surrender to a new way of doing things because our mind does not want to give up its old ways of thinking. At times I would look at my life and feel so hopeless because I would once again view it through the eyes of my filter system.

Finances were always challenging for me; no matter how much or how little money I made, I was always a dollar short and a day late. I read books on abundance and did positive affirmations. I budgeted, went bankrupt, recovered, had more money than I needed, only to find myself over my head in debt again. My mind continued to deal with money in its same old habitual fashion. No matter what I did, I couldn't seem to change the results I kept getting.

One day I changed my Intent and decided I was going to make money my friend instead of an adversary. I sat down and invited it to join me in developing a new kind of relationship. I literally saw money as a rather hefty, green man that looked like the Michelin tire man. We had a long talk, I felt good about it, and knew things would change. And they did; all hell broke loose. My old methods of juggling my bills, denying reality, and living with the hope that everything would be all right simply stopped working.

I was in a tailspin. I had to stop thinking and handling money the same way I always had. I had to learn how to think about money in concrete, practical, non-metaphysical terms. I was never so confused and frustrated in my entire life. My little self was enraged; she fought, kicked, and screamed. All my life I had mortgaged my future to pay for today. I had set my Intent to make money my friend and I had to make friends with money.

I found someone to teach me a new way to think and surrendered my finances to her guidance. I was not a very willing student at times. It was amusing really. Almost every thought I had about money was distorted by my old filter system. I would think I understood a concept, run it by my counselor, and find out after arguing rather vehemently for my limitations that I wasn't thinking clearly again. It was like learning a new language, but once I learned it money no longer ruined or ruled my life. I could breathe again and enjoy spending, saving, and sharing money in a caring and thoughtful manner. It was extremely liberating.

When we set our Intent to change something, it will change; we're just not in charge of how it changes. When

I set my Intent around money I had no idea how the process would look. I'm not sure what I expected, but certainly not what happened. The results, however, were far better than I ever anticipated. Money became a tool, a medium of exchange, and a loving, supportive friend. I gained control, my money went further, and I was able to develop a deeper sense of integrity.

IMAGINE

Spend some time out in nature. Just walk around and let yourself feel. When you are relaxed and comfortable, find a place to sit where you won't be disturbed and let yourself melt into the ground. Literally imagine yourself becoming one with the earth and let go.

Surrender is a process of letting go of our filter system. We have to repeat it over and over again until the surrender, rather than resistance, comes naturally. Whether the process is hard or easy depends upon what we tell ourselves. I look at surrendering to my Intent as a process of remembering and forgetting so I can remember again. I set my Intent; my life and my choices begin to change, I start listening to my filter system, and I forget my Intent to change my Intent.

Then I start getting the same old results, which reminds me that I am changing my Intent.

If I judge my progress or myself I only slow myself down. If I remember to relax and refocus as soon as possible, eventually I will remain on purpose all the time.

When you surrender the will of your little self to the Intent of your spiritual self, your healing journey will become much easier. At first, life will often become harder because you have to learn how to make new choices. Your small self may be terrified of being wrong or of taking the risk to be completely vulnerable, yet that is what your spirit will require. Being in alignment with your spirit demands absolute honesty, integrity, and vulnerability.

Your spiritual self only wants to fully experience its divinity; it wants to experience personal freedom in the most profound sense. It wants to break free of illusions and see the world through the eyes of angels; it wants to remember and see the world though the eyes of love. When you do that the sense of joy is beyond description and suddenly your small self's definition of happiness no longer matters. From the perspective of your spiritual self, happiness lies beyond your limitations and not safely surrounded by them.

THE GOALS BEYOND THE GOALS

When you set your Intent upon something, you will find that it comes to you because it is already within you. When you have a goal to attain, you are seeking something external, and will be disappointed. Let me explain.

In dominion, where we are all part of the circle of life, there really are no external goals. As soon as we start focusing on goals, we lose sight of what's really important and we step back into domination. In dominion everything is part of the whole, so goals in that context don't really make sense. Viewing life as an opportunity to

LET GO

Hold a pencil in your hand with your fingers tightly curled around it and your palm facing upward. There are two ways to let go of, or surrender the pencil: In one you merely uncurl your fingers, but you still have the pencil. In the other, you turn your hand over, open your fingers, and the pencil falls to the ground. Practice both ways of surrendering the pencil and notice how you feel. Write about your concept of surrendering.

experience what you are and what you're not, so you can remember your true self, does away with the need for goals. If you make remembering who you are a goal, making it a goal puts it beyond your reach. By setting goals, we're making the very thing we desire unattainable.

Goals in the traditional sense preclude embracing the object or objective. If you want a relationship in order to feel complete it implies you're incomplete. If instead you embrace the feeling you want to create, your world will mirror its existence in your life.

The grass truly isn't greener on the other side. Our happiness isn't dependent upon achieving goals. Allow your world to be big enough to make the other side a part of yourself and then you already have the greenest grass, so you don't have to go looking for it. The way our mind thinks about goals actually stops us from reaching goals. They remain elusive. Our mind thinks in terms of separation and domination, wherein we are perpetually in conflict. From the perspective of domination, "over there" and "over here" are two entirely separate things. From the perspective of our spirit and dominion everything is one; we can allow our world to be big enough to include everything.

ASK YOURSELF

What have your goals been in the past? How could you incorporate them into your life so they are no longer goals but become part of your life instead? How could you make them part of your Intent?

If you want to be happy, you have already succeeded in creating the desire to be happy. If you embrace happiness you will actually get to experience happiness instead of merely experiencing the desire to be happy. Whatever the object of your goal is, embrace it instead and it will be yours; make it a goal and it will elude you.

You wouldn't desire kindness or compassion unless you already had it within you. You can't see what doesn't already exist within you. In interviews with serial killers it became evident that they were unable to experience compassion. They didn't desire it because they didn't have it and they thought sensitivity was a sign of weakness.

Goals imply something exists beyond yourself. And nothing does, because you are one with the entire universe. You can't exclude anything if you are part of infinity. So if there is something you think is beyond you, realize it is already within you. Knowing that you already have something within yourself makes it much easier for you to allow it to appear in your physical reality.

Goals really do limit your experience of life. A far better way to move forward in your life is to ask yourself what you really want to create at any given moment. Ask yourself what you want to experience and then decide if you're willing to do whatever is necessary to experience it.

Setting your Intent works far better than setting goals. Intent can be called the energy behind your creation. So when you set your Intent you don't limit your experience; you actually open yourself up to more possibilities. When you set a goal it is much more fixed. Goals are very comfortable to your rational, linear mind. They are part of your filter system. Intent is connected with your spirit and is beyond your mind's control. Your mind can understand goals, but it often has a hard time fully grasping the concept of Intent.

REFLECT

Review your definition of personal freedom. What Intent would create that result? Is that honestly your Intent now?

One way to think of Intent is to think of it as the goal beyond the goal. And if you want to fully release your filter system you must allow yourself to move beyond the need to have goals. Goals are a box in which we place our awareness and limit the possibilities which, as we know, make our minds feel safe.

Moving beyond goals will push you to use all the tools we've talked about in this book. Living your life based on these concepts forces you to step out of the box created by society and allows you to live beyond its limitations.

TEACHING STORY

The Villagers Find Abundance

It had been a short, cold summer. The frost had come early and many were afraid that there wouldn't be enough food for the winter. A heaviness settled over the village and people walked hurriedly, bent over, wrapped in their blankets, not even looking at each other. Fear filled their hearts and tempers were short. The Grandmother was saddened; her heart hurt as she saw the beautiful seeds of love dying.

The talk of war started gradually, first with the young braves. They complained about how their neighbors were killing their deer and picking their berries. At first the others laughed because everyone knew the deer and berries belonged to the Great Spirit. But the talk of war soon took on a life of its own. It was a way for many of the people to channel their fear.

The old women heard the talk and wept silently at night. They knew firsthand the pain of war. They had lost many sons and husbands over the years but war had not visited their village since the Grandmother had come to live with them. One by one they came and sat at the Grandmother's fire; they talked about their fears, and asked the Grandmother what they could do.

"Forget your fear, walk in love. Look at the way others walk through the village. Walk not in fear. Share your love and your light as you move through the village; look at each person you pass and bless them. Share what you have, know that the Great Spirit will provide."

The old women left muttering to themselves. It was easy for the Grandmother to say; they knew death waited for all of them this winter. Their hearts were too full of fear to heed her words.

The talk of war continued to spread. People no longer shared their meals and families built their fires alone.

The hunters went out and came back empty handed. They cursed their luck and muttered in anger about the neighboring villages. They knew the spirits of the land were against them and that many would starve during the long winter ahead. The grumbling spread throughout the village.

Finally the elders called a council meeting. The young warriors stood outside, their faces filled with anticipation and fear. War was the answer and they all knew it. They would raid their neighbors, kill them, and take the food that had been stolen from their lands.

The meeting had been going on for most of the evening. The energy of war filled the air and the crowd was thick around the gathering place. There was barely room to move, when suddenly the crowd began to part.

The Grandmother walked slowly and deliberately toward the meeting place. As always her eyes were filled with love but there was a sadness and a determination few had ever seen before.

A murmur went through the crowd of women and young warriors as she lifted the skin covering the meeting room door. Women weren't allowed in the council meeting but no one dared stop her—she was, after all, the Grandmother.

The men fell silent as she entered. She looked around the room, meeting the eyes of everyone present, and she walked over to the Chief and stood in front of him. She looked deep into his eyes, then turned, and faced the fire as she raised her arms in prayer. The fire crackled, growing brighter by the moment, and the wind outside began to howl.

"I call upon the power of love. May only love be present here and may its light wash away any illusion of anger, hatred, or fear. I call upon the ancestors and all those who have gone before us or will come after us. May their wisdom and light be present here as well."

The air began to shimmer and the people could feel the loving presence of the Great Spirit. The Grandmother stood in silence, her eyes closed, and her hands open facing the sky.

When she finally spoke her voice was filled with gentleness and power. "What is it you want to create? Why did you gather here tonight? Will war really solve your dilemma?"

Everyone started talking at once. The voices of fear were loud and raucous. The Chief stood up and everyone fell silent.

"Grandmother, you know we don't have enough food for the winter and our neighbors kill our deer. We must protect our village. We must survive."

The Grandmother slowly turned and looked at the Chief.

"At what price?"

The Chief began to speak and the Grandmother silenced him. No one silenced the Chief. When he again tried to speak she turned and looked at him. Her eyes were full of fire. His mouth continued to move but he couldn't utter a single word.

"I said silence. I have enjoyed your loving hospitality for many moons. I have never interfered with tribal matters, but you have gone too far. Do you remember nothing I taught you? Do you so easily throw away the gifts of love? This village has grown and prospered because of the love you so freely shared. Do you love only when you feel safe? Do you turn your back on love as soon as fear starts whispering in your ear? Do you believe your eyes instead of your heart? Everything in your life is a gift freely given. If you try to hold on in fear it dissolves and you are left with nothing but your fear. Is that what you want?"

She looked around and stood before Gray Wolf. He had fear in his eyes and war in his heart.

"What is it you want to create with this war of yours? What is your intent, Gray Wolf?"

"I want to feed my family and take back what is rightly ours."

"Why do you want to feed your family, Gray Wolf?"

"That is a silly question, old woman; because I love them."

"So your intent is to show your love to your family by killing other families?"

She looked deeply into his eyes and touched his heart with her love. For a moment he had seen through her eyes and he saw what was really in his heart. He looked away in shame.

She looked around the circle and the men all lowered their eyes. They too had seen what was in their hearts and they were ashamed they had so easily surrendered to fear.

"If your intent is to love your families, love. Love everyone—especially your neighbors. If you let love be your guide you will always have enough. Fear causes starvation. Love never will. Give thanks for your blessings, bless your neighbor, share your bounty, and live in love.

"Your intent to love must be followed by loving actions. Love expands, fear contracts. If your intent is to love, be fearless in all you do, both in thought and in deed.

"Have you ever seen me want for anything? Have you ever seen me do anything but love? Would love deny you anything? My food barrels are full and yours will be too as soon as you open up your hearts and share. Give in love, without fear, and you will always have enough. As soon as fear infects your thinking you can be sure that scarcity will begin to rule your life."

The Grandmother turned and walked out of the room. The young warriors were surprised when the Chief emerged a little later and ordered everyone to begin preparations for a great feast. All the villagers returned to their homes and took stock of what they could contribute.

The next day the neighboring villages were all summoned to share in their bounty. Laughter filled the village again, there was plenty of food for everyone, and the Grandmother smiled as the Chief said the blessing. He talked about love and sharing. He talked about always having enough as long as your intent was to walk in love.

The village shared their food with many starving people that winter. Their storerooms were always full. Anyone who came to their village was offered a place by their hearths and given all they could eat. They were sent away with a full stomach, a heart full of love, and all the food they could carry to take back to their families. Many learned the lesson of love and intent that winter.

PART FIVE

Personal Freedom

Peaceful, joyous, loving, non-judgmental—do these words describe your free self, the person you believe that you can be? Each of us has our own concept of personal freedom. Regardless of your definition, the Toltec Masteries can help you live in your state of personal freedom.

For me, personal freedom is the ability to respond freely to the present moment. It is the ability to respond to what really is, rather than to my filter system's interpretation of what is happening. When I am fully present in the moment, I'm unfettered by the past and all the emotional garbage I've collected there.

Life can be a fun-filled adventure once you learn how to change your thought process. This is a path that takes discipline and dedication, but it is also a path that leads away from pain and suffering. It is a path that leads toward personal freedom. In a state of personal freedom I have the ability to act and remain centered regardless of what is going on around me. As I choose what actions to take, I continue to feel at peace, safe, and loved, and I know that everything will work out. I am free to do whatever I want at any given moment, I am no longer bound by my fears, and I truly have choices. The past no longer haunts me nor am I afraid of the future. I am truly living in the moment.

What is your definition of personal freedom? What would personal freedom look like for you? What would your life be like if you were totally free? Your answers to these questions may change over time. Revisit them often and allow your answers to grow and expand as you do.

CHAPTER ELEVEN

The Secret to Being Happy

If your definition of personal freedom resembles mine, it includes the ability to create whatever you want whenever you want it. The secret to being happy is wanting what you have.

We always create exactly what we want; we just don't want the results once we get them. Buddha said that the root of all our unhappiness comes from our desires and our attachments. Release those and you will find happiness.

If you want to be happy just be happy. Getting to the point where you can be happy sometimes takes effort and the willingness to make new choices. Your happiness resides completely within your mind. No external event or person can make you happy. The only thing that can make you happy is what you decide to tell yourself about life. The irony is that you don't have to change one thing about yourself, the world, or your life to be happy.

TAKE AN INVENTORY

Make a list of everything you like to do and that you consider fun. Cross off any self-destructive activities. Do at least one thing on the list every week.

If you really want to experience happiness, then you must be willing to change what you tell yourself and the way you view yourself. As long as you continue to judge anything about yourself, life, or other people's behaviors, happiness will remain elusive. Happiness, as with anything else in your life, is merely a choice; we just think it exists beyond us so we struggle to get it. Happiness can be yours right now just by deciding to be happy. Your mind might not get with the program right away; it might offer its opinions about what happiness is and you can choose to listen or not.

Most of us begin exploring spirituality because we are unhappy; we decide to do our emotional healing because we are in pain; we start looking at our belief systems because we don't like the results we are getting. I have seldom had anyone come to me and say, "I'm happy, my life is good, I just know I could be happier." Most people move away from pain rather than toward greater pleasure, but the results are very different.

DEFINE HAPPINESS

How do you define happiness? What are you willing to do in order to experience it on a regular basis?

As I've said earlier in this book, whatever you focus your attention on is what you get more of. So if you are constantly moving away from pain you will get more pain to move away from. What would it look like in your life if you started moving toward pleasure? What if instead of concentrating on what you want to change about yourself or your life, you concentrate on how you'd like to be?

You must choose what your creation will be rather than simply wanting to create something. If you want something, you've already succeeded at wanting it, so you're done.

Wanting to change something is very different from having changed it. You must generate the feeling of *having* rather than *desiring* to have. If you desire something your Intent is to desire it, and you'll never get any further than the desire.

I believe that the real key to happiness is releasing judgment and being grateful for everything, both for what is in your life and for what is not. Gratitude allows you to see with clarity and it allows you to be happy and feel connected to your spirit regardless of the circumstances. If your Intent is to be grateful, happiness will be a fringe benefit. And gratitude is much more possible when you surrender the will of your small self to the Intent of your spiritual self. It is the desires generated by your filter system that prevent you from feeling a sense of gratitude for all of your experiences.

As you've probably guessed, from my perspective, it is really all between your ears. This whole universe resides in your mind. Free your mind of limitations and you free yourself. You really can be as happy as you make up your mind to be. It is my wish for you that you do whatever is necessary to clear out your filter system and set yourself free. Be gentle with yourself, honor your process, and above all else love yourself just the way you are right here and right now.

TEACHING STORY

Embracing the Moment

Summer had just arrived and the hen was excited about her new brood. She had been sitting on the eggs for several days when she noticed an egg a few feet from the nest. It took a great deal of effort but at last she managed to roll it back into the nest and move it close to the others to keep it warm. She noticed that it was larger than the rest and a slightly different color but she sat lovingly on it anyway.

As each of her chicks hatched she clucked and cooed at them so they would always recognize her voice. The large egg seemed to take a long time to hatch and the chick didn't want to follow her at first. Grasshoppers were plentiful and it was the only thing the strange chick wanted to eat.

After a few weeks the new chick was larger than all the rest. She looked funny and out of place. She grew and grew. She learned to scratch and eat like the others, but in her heart she never felt like she belonged.

One day Grandfather eagle flew over the chicken coop. As soon his shadow passed over the yard all the chickens scattered, except for the young chick. The young chick stood in the shadows and watched as the Grandfather landed on one of the fence posts. He was magnificent, so proud and bold. His white head glistened in the sunlight. He looked steadily at the young chick as she hid in the shadows.

"Come here, child."

The chick hesitated; her mother clucked loudly, warning her not to go. She called loudly for her to come back into the coop.

"Don't be afraid, I won't hurt you."

The chick wavered for a moment before she ran for safety. Her heart was pounding as she tried valiantly to fit under her mother's protective wing.

"Child, you don't belong here. Your fear rules your mind. You can't see who and what you really are. I will be back and we will talk again."

With that the Grandfather eagle flew off to his home in the mountains. Each afternoon he came back and talked to the frightened chick. After he'd leave her mother would scold her for listening to his lies. The chick was confused; she wasn't sure why he kept coming back.

One day the Grandfather asked her to join him in the sky. She only laughed.

"I can't fly, I am only a chicken."

"No, you are not, my child. You are an eagle just like me. You have been scratching around for so long you have forgotten. Your heart is full of fear. Your mind may believe you're a chicken but you're not. Come and fly with me. Listen not to the fear that fills your mind; listen instead to your spirit. Let your spirit set you free."

Once again fear got the best of her and she ran for the safety of the coop. But that night, resting on her perch, she looked up at the stars and prayed. She asked the Great Spirit to help her know the truth.

Days went by but the Grandfather failed to appear. One day, when she had given up all hope of ever seeing him again, he arrived. This time there was a young eagle with him. As she looked at the young eagle she saw a reflection of herself sitting there. The Grandfather had been right; she was an eagle. Her heart soared, fear lost its grip, and what her mind said no longer mattered. She flapped her wings and found herself soaring among the clouds. At last she was free to be herself.

She looked at the Grandfather as he soared ahead of her and said a prayer of thanks to the Great Spirit. She looked down at the chicken coop far below and thanked her mother for her love. She would love her young with the same gentleness and caring her mother had always shown her. She would miss her family but at last she had found herself.

CHAPTER TWELVE

Staying on the Path

Finding your personal freedom is not a simple task. You will be confused at times, you'll find that you've taken two steps back for each step forward, and at times you will want to give up.

When people study with me, I can remind them to be gentle with themselves when they are struggling. When they are in emotional turmoil I can remind them to love themselves and embrace their discomfort. If you do nothing else, remember to accept where you are, embrace it, love it, and then choose again. Your process is your process.

Comparing yourself to anyone else serves no purpose. As soon as you use comparisons your filter system is in control and you're once again back in the paradigm of domination. Just be gentle with yourself as you learn to live your life from a place of dominion.

Many people find that one of their biggest obstacles in attaining their personal freedom is finding forgiveness for, and acceptance of, those who they believe have wronged them. Once we fully let go of all of our attachment to the past, to our filter system, and to our personal myth, there is no longer any need for forgiveness. We realize that no one did anything to us in the first place so we don't have anything or anyone to forgive. Getting to that point is akin to achieving enlightenment, so until we get there forgiveness is a very useful tool.

We forgive not for others but for ourselves. As long as we hold onto a judgment about someone else or his or her behavior we're enslaved by that part of our filter system. We'll never be free until we can forgive and let go. How do you forgive someone? Forgiveness is a definite process, and the deeper the wound, the longer the process tends to be. Remember that the emotional traumas we go through are always caused by our preexisting wound, not by someone else's behavior. If we hadn't been wounded in the first place their behavior wouldn't have bothered us, or they would've decided to play with someone else instead. Remember you didn't make them do it; don't let your mind blame yourself for their behavior.

TAKE FIVE

Spend five minutes at the beginning of each day remembering that we all have the same need to be happy and loved and that we are all connected to each other.

Spend five minutes cherishing yourself and others. Let go of judgments. Breathe in cherishing yourself, and breathe out cherishing others. If the faces of people you are having difficulty with appear, cherish them as well.

During the day, extend that attitude to everyone you meet—we are all the same, so cherish yourself and others. Do it with the grocery store clerk, the client, your family, your coworkers, the person who cuts you off in traffic, the person who has more items than allowed in the check-out line.

Once you have an emotional reaction it's too late not to have one, so the first step is to acknowledge your emotions. If you believe it will help you, you may write a series of letters that you don't send to whoever your mind says is triggering the emotions. Let your emotions flow as you write these letters; say it all. Eventually they will help you see your beliefs and your filters. Recapitulating the event will also help.

I find praying often helps me release my feelings toward a person. I may start out by asking with a bit of anger that the person gets everything they deserve, but eventually I can ask that their lives be filled with love and all the blessings I would wish for myself. Once I finally can say that and honestly mean it, I've truly let go.

One of the spiritual paradoxes is that there isn't really anything to forgive because the events aren't real. But in order to be free of the past and release it we have to forgive and to accept what was.

The most important person to forgive is yourself. You're perfect just the way you are and your life is perfect too. When I first realized I was the creative force in my life, I judged myself terribly. I forgot that my creation, my life, was my best attempt to release my limitations. In order to judge myself or anyone else I had to move back into domination where right and wrong, good and evil exist. But as you now know, the path to freedom requires us to admit where we are, forgive others and ourselves, and then make a new series of choices.

The only thing that is real is the energy I call love or God, the Great Spirit, or the creator. Behind the illusion we call life is the energy that makes it all seem real.

So what would seem to be of utmost importance is our connection to and our relationship with that energy. There are many ways to connect with that energy such as meditation, prayer, taking a walk in nature, breathing, and setting your Intent to connect. One of my favorite methods is to perform a ceremony.

A ceremony is a sacred act performed with the Intent of connecting to the creative force of the universe. Ceremonies come in many shapes and sizes. They can be a wonderful, magical, and sacred experience that can affect your life in the most profound manner.

There is no rigid formula for performing a ceremony. I suggest you find a place that feels sacred to you where you won't be disturbed. It can be in your home, out in nature, or any place that feels "right" to you. You can perform a ceremony in the midst of chaos if you want to—the location doesn't really matter, your Intent does. There are ceremonies of creation, of release, of forgiveness, or of thanks. Anything can be made into a ceremony and as a society we have a variety of them, such as marriages, funerals, and ordinations. You can have a ceremony alone, with others, or for others.

What significance do you want the ceremony to have in your life? Decide where you want to have it, what elements you want to include, and who you want to have there.

I always open a ceremony with a prayer that assists me in setting my Intent. I end with a prayer as a form of closure. What I do in between depends upon what the ceremony is for and where I am. I often perform my ceremonies on the beach and make lighting a bonfire part of them. As long as it feels right to you and assists you in connecting with the love, that's all that really matters.

Opening Prayer

Great Spirit, I give thanks for this opportunity to stand in the presence of your love. I call upon the energy of the ancestors and all those who have gone before me and all those who will come after me. Guide me and direct me. May only love and light be present here. May all present here feel your love. I call upon the four directions, the north, south, east, and west. I call upon the elements of this beautiful planet: I call upon the wind, the water, the fire, and the earth. I call upon the earth mother to hold us lovingly in her embrace. May the energy we generate here today be used to heal the planet and all those who reside upon it. I give thanks for this time of sharing, this time of healing, and this time of power. So it has been asked for so it will be received.

Closing Prayer

Great Spirit, I give thanks. I give thanks for all the gifts that have been received and will be received. May the healing that took place here unfold gently and lovingly in our lives. May we use the love so freely given in love. I give thanks to the four directions, to the elements, and to the ancestors. I give thanks for all those who came here to be of service this day. May all who came here be blessed and walk in the light now and always. I give thanks and say amen.

In some ceremonies, I ask participants to write letters and then burn them. You might want to write two letters, one about things you want to let go of and one about what you want to create. I sometimes hand out herbs and have people throw them in the fire. I use one set of herbs for release and one set for creation. I've found that a powerful ceremony for many people is to decorate a stick with everything they want to let go of on it and then burn it.

There are lots of other symbolic actions you can incorporate into a ceremony. You can bury things, throw non-polluting things in the water, mail letters addressed to God, dance, sing, or drum. The only limit is your imagination. Do it with Intent, with sacredness, and miracles will happen.

Ceremonies are very powerful. Often the more powerful a ceremony is the more unsettling it can be. If you decide to let go of something, all your resistance to releasing it is apt to arise in you. If you find yourself disturbed after a ceremony, use the tools of the Toltecs to embrace and understand the issues. As with anything else, be gentle with yourself.

The further you walk along the path to freedom, the clearer it will be to you that you are not alone. There is an old Yoruba proverb that says, "If we stand tall it is because we stand on the shoulders of many ancestors." All you have to do is reach out with your heart and other seekers will be there for you.

Make sure you develop a loving, nurturing inner voice to replace the voices of the judge and victim. Take the time to develop the ability to say positive, encouraging, and uplifting statements to yourself. I made a list of things to say and put it in the back of my journal and on my mirror. I also bought several packages of colored index cards. I wrote down quotes, insights, and anything I knew would help. I carried them everywhere I went and in spare moments I would read them like flashcards. You are learning a new language, the language of love. It is a language your filter system can't speak, so make those flashcards a memory aid to help you learn the new vocabulary.

And don't forget to make time to meditate. A wonderful meditation to do just before you go to sleep or as soon as you wake up in the morning is Meditation Four in Appendix A. Use it often until you really know you are the most precious gift there is and you can release your small self and speak from your heart.

I wish for you great happiness and joy. Let your process be a gentle one filled with love, curiosity, and wonder. You are at an exciting point in your life. Let yourself fully enjoy the experience; it is the only time you will pass this way, so fully embrace it.

The only regret I have about my studies is that I didn't allow myself to enjoy every minute of them. I always wanted to be just a little further along so I missed the gift of being right where I was. Life is only a series of moments in which we get to be right where we are or not. That's our choice, moment by moment, we can be where we are and enjoy it, or we can be where we are, pretend we're not, judge it, and miss all the joy. Be where you are—you are there anyway. I have learned to be where I am and enjoy each moment—it is a gift best savored fully.

Remember that you are a divine being living in dominion with everyone and everything. Let yourself love and be loved. Do things every day that feed your soul, spend time out in nature, talk to a tree, meditate, write, change your habits and routines, and above all else, be gentle with yourself. Talk to your spirit, ask your future self for help, and let yourself live fully and passionately. Take the time to create a definition of personal freedom that makes your heart sing.

TEACHING STORY

The Past Helps Heal the Future

The wind howled and the snow danced in ever-diminishing circles around the lonely pine tree. The snow crunched underfoot as the Grandmother walked toward the ridge. She wondered why she had been called out on that night. She pulled the blanket tighter about her as she crested the hill. The wind was fierce as she looked over the cliff. The village stood silently in the valley below. After all these years she knew better than to resist the call of her inner voice.

She nestled down onto a rock ledge and with a brush of her hand knocked the snow off a young tree bent in half from the weight of the snow. She smiled as it stood up straight and bobbed back and forth. She could feel the little tree's gratitude.

The Grandmother took a deep breath and gave thanks. As a fresh gust of wind rushed up from the valley her chant blended with it. Off in the distance she could hear a woman crying.

She closed her eyes and immediately had a vision of a young woman. The Grandmother found herself standing in a cave. The young woman was lying on a small blanket shivering. She was obviously in a great deal of pain. The Grandmother reached out and placed her hands on the young woman's swollen leg. Her skin was hot and dry. The woman's spirit was lost in a dream, wandering around chanting and asking the Great Spirit for help.

The Grandmother found some cool water and gently washed the woman's face. For a moment the Grandmother was shocked—she was looking at herself as a young girl. She remembered her pain and the kindness of the old woman who had saved her life. She smiled as she remembered the wisdom so freely given and how the old woman's love had healed her heart. She reached down into her medicine bag and removed some herbs.

With prayers of love and thanksgiving she prepared a poultice to remove the poison. With great care she cut open the wound. For days she tended her younger self. She chanted and prayed. When she closed her eyes she saw many paths leading away from that cave. Down one of the paths was darkness and death. Down others there were lives that held very little joy. And down one of those paths she lived in a wonderful village filled with love.

The Grandmother stood and watched. She stood in a place between time, filled with the energy of creation. It was a place where only possibilities lived. None of the paths were more real than the next and although they all existed, none of them existed. She always knew time wasn't real but she never realized so many lives existed at once. She allowed her consciousness to drift down some of the paths and looked back to see what decisions she'd made.

The Grandmother noticed her heart remained closed in most of those other lives, especially the ones without joy. In one of them she still taught children but they didn't love her. She constantly pointed out their faults so they would do things right and avoid being hurt. But she taught them fear instead of love so they couldn't feel joy; what greater hurt could there be?

She could see her own fear reflected in her words. She realized that every time she judged someone it was because of the fear and judgment within her own heart. As she looked inside her heart she saw that she really believed she was helping them, training them to do a better job. She was saddened; that self had no idea how hurtful her words were. She didn't see her words as critical, but she had hurt those she had tried so hard to love.

As she walked down another path she found herself alone in the desert, wandering. This self prayed a lot and spent her life trying to connect with the Great Spirit. She would wander into villages, healing and teaching, but never letting anyone get close. Her heart was closed and she pined for the love of the Great Spirit.

In one life she was a mother to two young boys. She had never healed her wound and although she loved them very much, she could never show them her love. They grew up as bitter men unable to love; they preached war and hate to the other men.

She was so grateful she had made the choices she had. But what had made the difference? What had she told her younger self? What had the other selves not heard that this one had?

As she brewed some herbs for the young woman she tried to remember the old woman's words, her own words yet to be spoken. What had the old woman told her so many years before that had removed all the pain from her heart?

A gust of wind brought the Grandmother back to the side of the mountain. She looked down over the cliff but the reassuring lights of her village were gone. She knew she must return to her younger self. She laughed to herself, what a strange thing time really is. At anytime we can reach out to our future self and ask for help.

As she drifted back into the vision she could feel the presence of her future self. She could feel herself standing on this very cliff setting her spirit free at the end of her days. The love was the thread that bound the past, present, and future together. Only the love was real.

She walked back into the cave just as her younger self was beginning to stir. Her fever had broken; she was weak, and still dazed, but she would recover. The

Grandmother walked over to the fire and poured them both a cup of tea.

"Drink this, little one, it will help you regain your strength."

"Who are you?"

"I am many things to many people. You could say I am just part of your dream. I come in love to help you heal and to free yourself of the past."

The younger woman drank the tea and fell asleep. When she awoke the Grandmother asked her if she was ready to hear the truth. The young woman's eyes narrowed; she cocked her head, and looked long and hard at the old woman. There was a light in the Grandmother's eyes and her touch was so warm and loving that she did want to hear more. She nodded and the Grandmother began.

"When we die, the love survives. You are a gifted healer, you know how to mend a broken bone or cure a lingering illness. Your Chief died because he had lost contact with his spirit. He had closed his heart so he could no longer love. Without love, even the strongest of us wither up and die.

"You came here to remind people to love one another. You came here to touch them with your kindness. You didn't come here to judge them or to fix them; you came here to teach them how to heal their hearts, but first you must heal your own.

"You must start by loving all the parts of yourself, even those dark places where anger and hatred live. You must love your judgment, you must love your shame, and you must love the weakest part of yourself with all your heart and all your soul. You must forgive yourself for every unkind thought and act in your life. You must love that small, scared part of your self that wants to lash out at others. You must love that part of you that protects you with judgment, anger, and control. Love, little one. Love every aspect of your being. You are perfect just the way you are, see yourself through the eyes of the Great Spirit, see yourself through the eyes of love."

The Grandmother reached out and gently held the younger self as she wept and released the pain of her self-imposed separation. They sat and talked for hours and the Grandmother's heart felt full. They talked about love and sharing, about the spirit that moved the earth and everything on it. The Grandmother shared her wisdom and love freely.

"Remember, little one, love fills the heart and satisfies all our wants and needs while fear leaves us feeling empty and always wanting more."

The young woman felt full too. She wanted to share that feeling of fullness with the entire world. When she looked around the old woman was gone but she knew she'd always be with her in her heart and she gave thanks.

The Grandmother looked down over the ridge and was grateful for all the people below waiting for her to return. So many moons ago she had gone back in time to heal herself; it had allowed her to love well and to teach many how to let love fill their hearts and set their spirits free. The snow had stopped and the wind had died down. The stars were bright as she began her way down into the valley.

IN CLOSING

Closing Prayer

May my intent be clear, pure, and loving.

May I always let my light shine brightly for all to see.

May I always be kind and loving to myself and others.

May I live so all may be uplifted by my presence.

May I be a blessing to all I meet and may all I meet bless me.

May any thought or deed that is less than loving contact the love and the light I truly am and be healed.

May I meet each day with a smile and may my heart always be filled with gratitude for the gift of the present moment.

May I walk always in love and light and laughter.

APPENDIX A

Guided Meditations

For all the following meditations find a place where you won't be disturbed for at least ten to fifteen minutes, unplug the phone, and if you have any pets, place them in another room. Take a few minutes to get really comfortable. If your clothes are tight, loosen them.

You could read these instructions over several times and just proceed, or you could read them into a tape recorder or have a friend read them to you. Relaxing takes time and practice. Don't judge your experience, just allow it to be.

MEDITATION ONE

Start by focusing your attention on your breathing. Notice how your breath feels as it comes in through your nose and how it feels as your lungs expand and contract. Take a few moments to notice your breathing, and while you are doing that, mentally give yourself permission to relax. As you continue to observe your breathing, notice how your chest relaxes. With each breath, allow your chest to relax. Let out a few heavy sighs, take a few really deep breaths, and let yourself relax. (long pause)

Settle back into your spirit; settle back into your body. Just follow your breath and let it flow into a gentle rhythm. Follow that rhythm; become that rhythm. Just let your breath relax you. Take some time to notice how good it feels to relax and let yourself sink into that feeling of relaxation. (pause)

Become *aware* of the muscles in the top of your head, around your scalp and your ears, and just gently invite them to relax. Focus your attention on the front of your face. Relax your face and all the tiny muscles around your eyes. Take a deep breath and give yourself permission to go deeper, to relax, to let go. Remind yourself that you could open your eyes any time you want, but it feels so good to relax that you just let go. Take a deep breath and go even deeper.

If your mind wanders, just allow that to relax you even more. Gently bring your attention back to your breathing and relax.

Relax your jaw; let your tongue fall to the floor of your mouth; allow your jaw to part slightly and just relax. Feel the relaxation floating down your spine; feel it go down vertebrae by vertebrae, relaxing you totally and completely. Feel your chest filling with a deep sense of relaxation. Feel your chest opening, relaxing, and letting go. Feel it moving down into your stomach. (pause)

Now feel it going down your legs and out your feet. Imagine yourself completely surrounded by a pink and green cloud that gently caresses your body. It flows around and through you. It is filled with the energy of peace and love and of deep relaxation. Allow the cloud to flow around you, gently caressing you until you are filled with a deep sense of peace. (pause)

As you breathe in the pink and green cloud imagine yourself being filled with love. Each time you inhale you are filled with more and more love. As you exhale your entire body relaxes. Relax, just breathe deeply, and relax.

Allow yourself to feel, really feel the love, the peace, and the relaxation. (long pause)

Imagine yourself walking along in the countryside. The air is warm and the wind is gently blowing. The birds are singing and the air smells fresh and clean. You feel totally at peace, relaxed, and safe. The sky is incredibly blue and there are beautiful, fluffy, white clouds floating by. The air smells so sweet. You take a deep breath to fill your lungs with its sweetness and your entire body relaxes. You feel so peaceful and relaxed. (pause)

You look up at the clouds and you notice how each one is different; each one is unique, yet perfect. You notice how easily the clouds drift across the sky. Even though each cloud is different they are all beautiful; each one is perfect in its own way. You just relax and watch the clouds. (pause)

As the clouds move across the sky it is easy to accept the way they move. They float effortlessly across the sky neither resisting nor judging their progress. Sometimes they bring rain; at other times they just float along causing shadows to flicker across the landscape. At times they are big and stormy and they obscure the sun, but the sun is still there just behind the clouds.

It is easy to accept the clouds just the way they are. It is easy to see their beauty and their perfection. For a moment let yourself become a cloud. Imagine yourself effortlessly floating through your life. Imagine viewing your life with the same peace and acceptance you felt for the clouds. Imagine that the events in your life are merely clouds floating by. Even in the darkest moments happiness is still there just behind the sadness.

Remember the perfection of the clouds, how easy it is to accept them just the way they are. Now let yourself know, at the core of your being, that you too are perfect. Just as you accepted the clouds, begin to accept yourself. Allow yourself to accept and love yourself, just as you are. (long pause)

Feel that sense of self-acceptance flowing through you, embracing you and filling you with a deep sense of peace and love. (pause)

When you are done, gently and lovingly bring yourself back to this room.

Take at least a few minutes to bring yourself back. Get up slowly and give yourself some time to become oriented to the room again. You might want to stretch gently and take a few deep breaths. Give yourself a few minutes to think about the following questions:

- How do you feel physically?
- How do you feel emotionally?
- Were you able to accept yourself?
- Did you find it hard to let go of any judgments you have about yourself?
- How does your body feel?

The more often you allow yourself to experience this or any other meditation, the easier it will become. Just notice any resistance you have to the process. Try to get in touch with the inner dialog, what it is you are telling yourself that is causing your resistance. Change that dialog and your experience will change. Tell yourself it is easy to follow the meditation and it will be.

Most importantly, honor your process and be gentle with yourself. And remember, you are perfect just the way you are. If you don't acknowledge your perfection now, no matter how much you change, no matter how perfect you become, you will never experience your perfection. So, allow yourself to be perfect moment by moment.

MEDITATION TWO

Remember to make sufficient time and space for yourself. It is normal for your mind to wander. If it does, lovingly and gently bring yourself back to the meditation.

Start by focusing your attention on your breathing. Notice your breath. Notice how it feels as it comes in through your nose and how it feels as your lungs expand and contract. Take a few moments to really notice your breathing and while you are doing that, mentally give yourself permission to relax. As you continue to observe your breathing, notice how your chest relaxes. With each breath allow your chest to relax. Let out a few heavy sighs, take a few deep breaths, and really let yourself relax. (long pause)

Settle back into your spirit; settle back into your body. Just follow your breath and let it flow into a gentle rhythm. Follow that rhythm; become that rhythm. Just let your breath relax you. Take some time to notice how good it feels to relax, and let yourself sink into that relaxation. (pause)

If your mind wanders, just allow that to relax you even more. Bring your attention back to your breathing and relax.

Focus your attention on your breathing. Notice where you feel your breath. Do you feel it in your nose, your

229

chest, or your stomach? Where do you feel your breath? Focus your attention on that part of your body and notice your breathing. Follow your breath as it goes in and out. (long pause)

Take a few deep breaths and give yourself permission to go deeper, to relax, to let go. Remind yourself that you could open your eyes any time you want, but it feels so good to relax that you just let go. Take a deep breath and go even deeper.

As you breathe in imagine yourself breathing in a feeling of peace and relaxation. Allow yourself to relax. If your mind wanders just bring yourself gently back to your breath. And relax. (pause)

You are standing in front of a magnificent temple. As you stand at the foot of the stairs, you notice how worn they are. Deep within you, you know this is a very ancient place of learning. It feels very old, very powerful, and very sacred. (pause)

As you begin to walk up the stairs, the guardians greet you. They welcome you warmly, and you feel a deep sense of love, peace, and safety. As you enter the temple, the wind lovingly caresses your face. In the center of the room is a beautiful fountain of many different colored lights. A caretaker gently leads you over to it and motions for you to step in. The colored light begins to fill your being. The light fills you and washes away any tension or cares. For a moment you are free of limitations.

You feel yourself being carried out of the fountain and lovingly placed on the altar. Light continues to flow through you, and you begin to dream. (pause)

You imagine what it would feel like if you were completely free. Picture yourself doing whatever you enjoy doing the most. (pause)

Imagine your life filled with joy. Picture all the things in life that bring you a feeling of joy. Imagine your life filled with those things. (pause)

Imagine your life filled with a deep sense of peace. Picture yourself in places and doing things that bring you a sense of peace. (pause)

Imagine yourself free of any limiting thoughts or beliefs. Imagine a world based on love, a world completely free of fear. You let go and let yourself fly. Imagine yourself effortlessly flying, soaring through the sky. Feel the wind; just feel the freedom. (long pause)

Now, imagine what your life would be like if your life was filled with feelings of peace and joy and freedom.

Imagine yourself feeling totally safe and loved. What if you knew life was limitless and you could have anything you want or need? How would your life be different? How would you act? How would you feel? How would you treat others? Let your imagination soar. (long pause)

When you are ready, take a few deep breaths and gently bring yourself back to the room.

- How did that feel?
- What thoughts did your mind have about the process?
- Did your mind tell you it wasn't possible? If so, how?
- Did your mind tell you that it was unreal or did it allow you to enjoy it?
- You might want to take a few minutes to write about what you want to create in your life. Allow your creation to be limitless.
- Seeing and feeling some of those feelings might take a bit of time and practice. Don't listen to your mind if it says it's impossible because not only is it possible, it is your birthright.

Appendix A

MEDITATION THREE

Take a few deep breaths and give yourself permission to relax. Focus your attention on your breathing. Really feel your breath as your chest and stomach rise and fall. (pause)

Relax your jaw. Allow your tongue to fall to the floor of your mouth. Imagine a feeling of relaxation starting at the top of your head and slowly flowing down your entire body. Feel it as it flows over your face, relaxing all the tiny muscles in and around your eyes. Relax your neck. See that feeling of relaxation as it gently swirls down your back, vertebra by vertebra. Feel the relaxation going out to each and every nerve and fiber of your entire body. (pause)

Take a deep breath and allow yourself to relax totally and completely. As you inhale, relax and inhale a deep sense of peace and relaxation. As you exhale, release anything unlike relaxation. Allow your consciousness to drift, let go, and imagine yourself floating peacefully down a river. You are lying on a huge rubber raft. The water is warm, there is a gentle breeze, and the sun flickers through the canopy of trees. You feel at peace and at one with yourself and with your surroundings.

The raft comes to rest on a beautiful sandy beach. There are two beings of pure, white light waiting for you. They

233

gently pick you up and carry you to shore. Their touch is very gentle and loving. You feel thoroughly loved and accepted just the way you are.

One of the beings looks deeply into your eyes and asks you if you are ready to let go of your limitations. You hesitate for a moment and the being gently touches your heart. You feel yourself being filled with a deep sense of love and self-acceptance. You feel yourself relaxing and going very deeply into the silence of your mind. Your mind's thoughts seem further and further away. Your mind and your filter system begin to melt like a giant block of ice. You sit in silence as you see it slowly dissolve, drip by drip. You feel more and more relaxed. (pause)

In the silence of your mind you hear a voice. At first you hear it dimly, way off in the distance, but as you relax the voice comes closer. It is the loveliest sound you've ever heard. After a moment you realize it's the voice of your own spirit; it's your soul. It is the energy that exists beyond your filter system, beyond your mind.

Your spirit reaches out and touches you and a feeling of warmth flows through your entire body. Allow your heart to open and let the love in. Take a deep breath and imagine your spirit holding you lovingly in its embrace. (pause)

Allow the connection to deepen. Allow yourself to feel the love. Ask for guidance, ask for help, and let go of your little self. Step fully and completely into the essence of who and what you are. Take a deep breath and let yourself fully embrace who and what you are. (long pause)

Whenever you're ready slowly and gently bring yourself back to the room.

Ask yourself:

- How did that feel?
- Did your mind resist letting go?
- What was it like to see your filter system dissolve?

As with any of the meditations, repetition makes it easier. If you find yourself thinking "I can't do that" or you have problems with any parts of the visualization, spend some time before you do the mediation again thinking of images that will work for you. Adding colors and textures sometimes helps.

The most important thing is to remember that this is just a game of let's pretend. In the meditation I suggest you experience something and you pretend you are experiencing it. It can be a mystical, magical experience if you allow it to be. If you find that you have a hard time visualizing an image or images, shift your focus away from the need to visualize "well." Just allow yourself to relax and let yourself enjoy the meditation. Allow for the possibility that it will be easy and it will. Don't try; just relax, and allow the experience to happen.

MEDITATION FOUR

Allow yourself to relax completely. Let go and relax. Focus your attention on the point in your body where you feel your breath. As you inhale, breathe in relaxation; as you exhale breathe out anything unlike relaxation. As you exhale, really let go. Let out a loud sigh and let go of everything and anything. (pause)

Imagine your heart beating gently in your chest, filling your body with oxygen and a deep sense of relaxation. Feel a deep sense of gratitude and love for being alive and having this opportunity to be who you are. With each beat of your heart allow yourself to go deeper and deeper and allow yourself to relax more fully and completely. Take a very deep breath and relax your chest and your shoulders. Slowly rotate your neck and feel all the muscles. Rotate your shoulders and feel each muscle as they move your shoulders and your neck. If you notice any tension just let it go as you breathe out and relax. (pause)

Yawn and relax your jaw and all the muscles in your face. Inhale deeply and relax. As you relax you will feel your mind as it slows down, grows quieter, and lets go. Any stray thoughts you have will only serve to relax you even more as you effortlessly watch them go by. (long pause)

You find yourself standing in a clearing in the middle
of an ancient forest. The air is warm and heavy with the
fresh smell of wet earth. The stars are shining brightly and
the wind swirls around the clearing filling your heart with
a deep yearning. The clearing glows and the air shimmers
as you walk toward the center of the clearing. The sound
of the leaves rustling is comforting and very relaxing.

As you stand in the center of the clearing, an old man
begins to walk toward you. His face is lined and his hands are
gnarled with age. He wears a long robe with many folds. You
look deeply into his eyes and you feel incredibly loved and
totally accepted. He smiles and welcomes you to his world. A
feeling of warmth and a deep sense of gratitude emanate
from him. You feel like you could get lost in his eyes. (pause)

He reaches out and lovingly touches your heart. You
find yourself getting warmer and warmer, you find yourself
filled with feelings of peace and love. With his other hand
he reaches into his robe and pulls out a beautiful crystal. He
holds it over his head, it sparkles brilliantly, and it begins to
pulse with a bright, white light. He places it over your heart
and you feel it as it merges with your spirit and your mind.

Suddenly you see your life through different eyes. You
see life through the eyes of love. You see and experience

your perfection. And you realize that you have been the gift in your life all along. You take a deep breath and let the feeling fill you. You laugh to yourself; there has never been anything wrong with you; your judgment and self-criticism have been the problems all along, and you let them go. It feels like a huge weight has been lifted off your shoulders; you feel freer than you could have ever imagined. You let the feelings of self-love and acceptance flow through you like a healing balm soothing and comforting you. (long pause)

The old man continues to look at you and smile. You could get lost in his eyes. He knows you and loves you dearly. He continues to hold his hand over your heart and you let go of more and more of your old emotional poison. He is there to help you heal and you let him. You let his love enter into the darkest parts of your being and you release the pain and suffering of lifetimes. You take deep breaths and let go at deeper and deeper levels.

You see an old woman step out of the shadows. She too touches your heart. They stand there together, looking lovingly at you, and each other. They are there for only one purpose, to love you and help you heal.

When they are done they nod at each other and smile. First the old woman stands in front of you and looks deeply into your eyes. Her voice is the most beautiful sound you have ever heard. She looks at you and says, "I am honored to be in your presence." Before you can speak she puts her finger over your lips and tells you to hold on to the love and not give it away with your words. She hugs you and then she is gone.

Next the old man stands in front of you and says, "I too am honored to be in your presence." His voice resonates through your entire body. You take a deep breath and take his words in. He smiles and before he leaves he reminds you that they will always be with you, right at the edge of your reality, waiting, and wanting to love you. Whenever you think of them you hear their voices reminding you, loving you. They are a part of you now and always.

You stand alone in the middle of the clearing and you are filled with love and peace. You are your true self and you know you are a gift, and you go forth into your life to share your light. (long pause)

Take your time getting up. You might want to put a sign on your mirror that says, "I'm honored to be in your presence." Read it often and speak it lovingly to yourself as you stand in front of the mirror and look directly into your eyes.

APPENDIX B

Glossary

Agreements—Consciously or unconsciously we make contracts or arrangements with the people in our lives and with the world itself. We have agreed to believe certain things and to act in a specified manner. If our parents believed intimacy was unsafe we may have agreed to believe that too. We may have an unconscious agreement with ourselves to remain unhappy. We are generally unaware of our agreements and yet they dictate most of our choices and our actions.

Assumptions—We often assume that we know what another person is thinking or feeling. We assume other people think the same way we do. We assume people mean the same thing we think they mean. When we take things for granted, when we make assumptions, we are on dangerous ground. As soon as we make an assumption we are dealing with our filter systems and not with reality.

Attention—Our attention is where we choose to focus our mind, thoughts, and actions. Whatever we focus our attention on we get more of. If we focus on fear we will get more fear. If we focus our attention on personal freedom we will create that as well.

Awareness—Awareness is our ability to see with clarity. It is one of the three Toltec Masteries. Awareness is a skill we develop as we become aware of and release our filter systems.

Beliefs—Beliefs are thoughts we have about reality that we think are accurate. We live our lives based on our beliefs and rarely question them because we believe them to be true. Our attachment to proving our beliefs true causes most of our limitations, pain, and emotional turmoil.

Ceremony—A ceremony is a sacred act. It can include a ritual, a blessing, a prayer, and an activity. It is a powerful way to connect with your divinity and universal energy. Ceremonies can be very personal and transformative. Generally they open and close with a prayer. How you fill up the space in between is up to you.

Dedication—Dedication is a deep commitment to yourself. Dedication can assist you in making certain activities non-negotiable, which will allow you to focus on what you really need to do.

Discipline—Discipline is the ability to stay focused on the task at hand, to make yourself do what you need to do, and to follow through on your commitments to yourself.

Domination—Domination is a paradigm or way of looking at the world that is very linear. It is based on duality, and on the concept that things are measurable. Our society exemplifies the viewpoint of domination, in which things are right or wrong, better than or less than, black or white. Domination encourages judgment, fear-based thinking, and group mentality.

Dominion—Dominion is a paradigm or way of looking at the world that is very inclusive. Symbolically, it is represented by a sphere. In dominion all people are part of the great circle of life. When we live life in dominion we realize people see things differently because we all see life from a different spot on the sphere. From a place of dominion it is much easier to embrace our limitations and change things. Dominion encourages love and individuality.

Filter system—Our filter systems are composed of our beliefs, agreements, assumptions, and definitions. We see the world dimly thorough our filter systems. It is like looking through a waterfall. Our vision of the world is severely distorted by our filter systems.

Intent—Intent is the third of the Toltec Masteries. In the purest sense, Intent is the energy of creation; it is how we create our experience of reality. Learning to surrender to your Intent is incredibly powerful and freeing.

Nagual—The spiritual aspect of our world; *nagual* is also used to refer to a teacher who has achieved personal freedom and is guiding other people in their quest to find personal freedom.

Path—Each of us has our own individual path. The Hawaiians say there are many paths to the top of the mountain, but the view from the top is the same regardless of what path you have taken.

Personal freedom—The definition for personal freedom is unique to each of us. It is something you define for yourself. For me, it is based on my ability to choose how I want to act in my life, instead of reacting to my filter system. Having a clear definition of what personal freedom means to you is important; it can help guide and direct your thoughts and actions.

Personal importance—Personal importance is a state of being disconnected from our essence. It is tied up with our filter systems and curtails our ability to make loving choices. Personal importance will try to convince you that it's not personal importance. It will lie to you and try to sell you a line. It will sacrifice anything to remain in control, including your health and your happiness.

Personal power—Personal power is in alignment with our spirit or true self. When we make decisions from our personal power they tend to be based on love. Personal power is a quiet, still voice that will make gentle suggestions. It will never annoy you or remind repeatedly. It is your gateway to freedom and true happiness.

Process—A process takes time and effort. It is ongoing and should be allowed to unfold in its own way.

Spiritual—Spiritual is anything that pertains to our spirit or the realm of the *nagual*. We are all spiritual beings having a physical experience.

Surrender—Surrender is a letting go and release of control.

Transformation—Transformation is the second of the Toltec Masteries. It is a method of viewing your life that assists you in seeing your filter system and in healing old wounds.

APPENDIX C

Suggested Reading

This is a list of a few of my favorite books. Many of the authors listed here have also written other excellent books. I recommend them as well. Books always seem to have a way of finding you when you need them.

Channeled

Bartholomew, Moore, M., et al. *I Come As A Brother: A Remembrance of Illusions.* High Mesa Press, 1986.

————. *Reflections of An Elder Brother: Awakening the Dream.* High Mesa Press, 1989.

Rodegast, Pat, et al. *Emmanuel's Book: A Manual for Living Comfortably in the Cosmos.* New York: Bantam Books, 1985.

———. *Emmanuel's Book II: The Choice for Love.* New York: Bantam Books, 1989.

———. *Emmanuel's Book III: What is An Angel Doing Here?* New York: Bantam Books, 1994.

Emotional Healing

Borysenko, Joan, Ph.D. *Fire in the Soul.* New York: Warner Books. 1993.

Friel, John and Linda. *Adult Children.* Deerfield Beach, FL: Health Communications, 1988.

Muller, Wayne. *Legacy of The Heart.* New York: Fireside, 1992.

Healing

Brennan, Barbara Ann. *Light Emerging: The Journey of Personal Healing.* New York: Bantam Books, 1993.

Hay, Louise L. *You Can Heal Your Life.* Carlsbad, CA: Hay House, Inc., 1984.

Joy, W. Brugh, M.D. *Joy's Way.* New York: Jeremy P. Tarcher, 1979.

King, Serge Kahili, Ph.D. *Instant Healing.* Los Angeles: Renaissance Books, 2000.

Kloss, Jethro. *Back to Eden.* Back to Eden Books, 1985.

Kraft, Dean and Rochelle. *A Touch of Hope.* New York: Berkley Books, 1999.

Myss, Caroline, Ph.D. *Anatomy of the Spirit.* New York: Three Rivers Press, 1996.

Rain, Mary Summer. *Earthway.* New York: Pocket Books, 1990.

Inspirational

Albom, Mitch. *Tuesdays with Morrie.* New York: Doubleday Books, 1997.

Bach, Richard. *Illusions.* New York: Delacorte Press/ Eleanor Friede, 1977.

Coelho, Paulo. *The Alchemist.* New York: Harper Collins, 1993.

Girzone, Joseph F. *Joshua.* New York: Macmillan, 1987.

Hanh, Thich Nhat. *Peace is Every Step.* New York: Bantam Books, 1991.

————. *Touching Peace.* Berkeley, CA: Parallax Press, 1992.

Kornfield, Jack. *A Path With Heart.* New York: Bantam
  Books, 1993.

Millman, Dan. *The Laws of Spirit.* Tiberon, CA: H J
  Kramer, Inc., 1995.

———. *Way of the Peaceful Warrior.* Tiberon, CA:
  H J Kramer, Inc., 1984.

Redfield, James. *The Celestine Prophecy.* New York: Warner
  Books, 1993.

Roberts, Jane. *The Oversoul Seven Trilogy.* San Rafael, CA:
  Amber-Allen Publishing, 1995.

Ruiz, don Miguel. *The Four Agreements: A Practical Guide to
  Personal Freedom from a Toltec Wisdom Book.* San Rafael,
  CA: Amber-Allen Publishing, 1997.

Walsch, Neale Donald, *Conversations With God: An
  Uncommon Dialogue (Book I).* New York: G P Putnam's
  Sons, 1995.

Williamson, Marianne. *A Return to Love.* New York:
  HarperCollins, 1992.

Prosperity

Ponder, Catherine. *The Dynamic Laws of Prosperity.* De Vorss,
  1984.

Roman, Sanaya, and Duane Packer. *Creating Money.*
Tiberon, CA: H J Kramer, Inc., 1988.

Relationships

Ruiz, don Miguel. *The Mastery of Love: A Practical Guide to the Art of Relationship.* San Rafael, CA: Amber-Allen Publishing, 2000.

Welwood, John. *Love and Awakening.* New York: Harper Collins, 1997.

Shamanism

Andrews, Lynn V. *Woman at the Edge of Two Worlds.* New York: HarperCollins, 1993.

Feather, Ken Eagle. *A Toltec Path.* Charlottesville, VA: Hampton Roads Publishing Co., 1995.

Gregg, Susan, Dr. *Dance of Power.* St. Paul, MN: Llewellyn Publications, 1993.

———. *Finding the Sacred Self.* St. Paul, MN: Llewellyn Publications, 1995.

King, Serge Kahili, Ph.D. *Mastering Your Hidden Self.* Wheaton, IL: Theosophical Publishing House, 1985.

————. *Urban Shaman.* New York: Fireside, 1990.

Sanchez, Victor. *The Teachings of Don Carlos.* Santa Fe, NM: Bear & Co., 1995.

Wabun, Sun Bear, and Barry Weinstock. *The Path of Power.* New York: Prentice Hall, 1987.

THANK YOU, READER

Don't hesitate to do whatever it takes to set yourself free with love and gentleness. Thank you so much for bringing this book into your life. If I can be of any further assistance, please feel free to contact me. I'd love to hear from you.

My e-mail address is sgregg@aloha.com

My Web site is www.aloha.com/~sgregg

Or you can write me (a self-addressed, stamped enve-lope would be greatly appreciated) at:

Dr. Susan Gregg
P.O. Box 910
Waimanalo, Hawaii 96795

I also conduct a discussion group that you might enjoy. It is a good place to meet like-minded individuals, ask ques-tions, and share your wisdom, love, and light. To subscribe, send a message to: toltecmastery-subscribe@egroups.com, or go to my Web site and click on the eGroups.com icon.

In love and light,

ABOUT THE AUTHOR

Susan Gregg was born in Queens, New York, and spent her teen years in rural Vermont. She earned her bachelor's degree in math at the University of Vermont. During her years of training in the Toltec way to happiness and peace, Gregg earned her doctorate in clinical hypnotherapy.

For many years Gregg has lived on the island of Oahu in Hawaii, where she maintains a private practice assisting clients in attaining their personal freedom. Gregg's previous books include *Dance of Power*, *Finding the Sacred Self*, and *The Complete Idiot's Guide to Spiritual Healing*.

Gregg lives with a collection of rescued and adopted animals. Muffy, her Pekingese, spends a good deal of time chasing cats, but is otherwise a good dog.